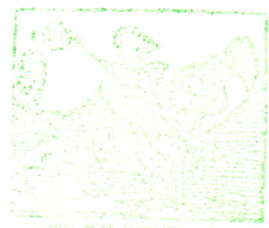

Also by Richard N. Goodwin

The American Condition

Promises to Keep: A Call for the New American Revolution

Remembering America: A Voice from the Sixties

The Sowers Seed: A Tribute to Adlai Stevenson

Triumph or Tragedy: Reflections on Vietnam

THE HINGE OF THE WORLD

A DRAMA

THE HINGE OF THE WORLD

IN WHICH

PROFESSOR GALILEO GALILEI,

CHIEF MATHEMATICIAN AND PHILOSOPHER TO HIS SERENE

HIGHNESS THE GRAND DUKE OF TUSCANY,

AND

HIS HOLINESS URBAN VIII,

BISHOP OF ROME,

BATTLE FOR THE SOUL OF THE WORLD

A DRAMA BY

RICHARD N. GOODWIN

FARRAR • STRAUS • GIROUX

NEW YORK

Farrar, Straus and Giroux
19 Union Square West, New York 10003

Copyright © 1998 by Richard N. Goodwin
All rights reserved
Distributed in Canada by Douglas & McIntyre Ltd.
Printed in the United States of America
Designed by Jonathan D. Lippincott
First edition, 1998

Library of Congress Cataloging-in-Publication Data
Goodwin, Richard N.
The hinge of the world : in which professor Galileo Galilei, chief mathematician and philosopher to His Serene Highness the Grand Duke of Tuscany, and His Holiness Urban VIII, Bishop of Rome, battle for the soul of the world : a drama / by Richard N. Goodwin. — 1st ed.
    p. cm.
ISBN 0-374-17002-9 (alk. paper)
1. Galilei, Galileo, 1564–1642—Drama. 2. Urban VIII, Pope, 1568–1644—Drama. 3. Religion and science—Drama. 4. Astronomers—Italy—Drama. 5. Popes—Drama. I. Title.
PS3557.O6235H56 1998
812'.54—dc21   97-32893

to the memory of Willam Shawn

and

to Roger Straus

Author's Note

In preparing this play for presentation in book form, I have included material intended to enhance a reader's comprehension and pleasure, material that might best be omitted from a stage production.

The heart of any stage presentation would be Act 3, which presents the direct confrontation between Galileo and Pope Urban VIII, the two most titanic egos of the seventeenth century. Some material from the first two acts would be necessary, of course, to permit a fuller understanding of the principal characters and issues of the drama, and to allow scope for pageantry. Just such a shortened script was used for a staged dramatic reading conducted at the Actors Studio.

I have given considerable thought to the Thirty Years' War as a sub-theme. It might, in performance, prove desirable to omit reference to the war, but on the other hand, the shifting fortunes of war had a great deal to do with the actions of the principal characters. This is a question more of stagecraft than of literature.

The characters and events depicted in this play are, for the most part, historically accurate. The conversations and arguments are imagined, derived from my own understanding of the men and the times.

THE HINGE OF THE WORLD

A DRAMA

CAST OF CHARACTERS
(in alphabetical order by the act in which they first appear)

ACT ONE

Maffeo Cardinal Barberini, Vatican Ambassador to France, later Pope Urban VIII
Roberto Cardinal Bellarmine, General of the Society of Jesus, Consultor of the Holy Office, Master of Controversial Questions, leading theologian
Giordano Bruno, a condemned heretic
Benedetto Castelli, a monk of Monte Cassino, student of Galileo
Monsignor Giovanni Ciampoli, Cardinal Barberini's assistant and closest friend, later Master of the Sacred Palace when the Cardinal becomes Pope Urban VIII
Ferdinand, King of Bohemia
Galileo Galilei
Marina Gamba, Galileo's mistress in Padua, mother of his three children
Sister Maria Celeste, Galileo's daughter
Marcantonio Mazzoleni, Galileo's assistant and resident technician
Pope Paul V
Philip, King of Spain
Duc de Richelieu (Armand du Plessis), Chief Minister to King Louis XIII of France
Gioan (Giovanni) Francesco Sagredo, a Venetian patrician, friend of Galileo
Filippo Salviatti, a noble of Florence, friend of Galileo
Dr. Santerre Santorio, a Venetian physician and friend of Galileo
Senators of the Venetian Republic

ACT TWO

Francesco Cardinal Barberini, Pope Urban VIII's nephew
Lorenzo Bernini, sculptor
Andrea Cigoli, Secretary of State to the Grand Duke
The Conspirators:
    Father Tommaso Caccini, a Dominican priest
    A Cardinal
    Ludovici delle Colombe, a professor of philosophy at the University of Pisa, leader of the anti-Galileo group among Tuscan academicians; later Simplicio
    Niccolo Lorini, a Dominican priest and a professor of ecclesiastical history at Florence
    Father Antonio Magini, a professor of mathematics at the University of Bologna
Cosimo II, Grand Duke of Tuscany
Father Horatio Grassi, a professor of mathematics at the Collegio Romano
Johannes Kepler, chief astronomer to the imperial court
Louis XIII, King of France
Lorenzo Magalotti, papal Secretary of State
Grand Duchess Marina Christina of Lorraine, mother of Grand Duke Cosimo
Mazzimedici, Archbishop of Florence
Francesco Niccolini, a friend of Cosimo's, later Tuscan Ambassador to the Papal States
Lorenzo Seghizi, Commissary-General of the Inquisition during Galileo's first visit to Rome
Marina Tedaldi, Galileo's mistress in Florence
Lord Wackher, a nobleman of Prague

ACT THREE

Cardinal Bentivoglio, Chief Inquisitor of the Holy Office
An Englishman
A Frenchman
Gustavus Adolphus, King of Sweden
B. Landini, a printer
Father Vincenzo Maculano (Firenzuola), Commissary-General of the Inquisition
Federigo Morosini, a Venetian patrician
François de Noailles, French Ambassador to the Papal States
General Oxenstierna, the King's second-in-command
Giacinto Stefani, Inquisitor-General of Florence

It is the first quarter of the seventeenth century. The Renaissance of three hundred years is virtually extinguished, its radiance crowded to the margins of Europe, where, on the stage of the Globe Theatre, men are making their final assaults on swiftly darkening Olympus.

On the Continent the armies of Europe are confronting one another in the first battles of the Thirty Years' War, whose convulsions will end forever any hope of reunifying the Christian world. Amid the turbulent clamors of war, a handful of men, scattered across Europe, are beginning to define nature by reason unconfined by belief. Among these creators of the modern world is the mathematician and philosopher Galileo Galilei, a citizen of Florence.

ACT ONE

(*The top level of the curtain displays a figure vaguely resembling Cardinal Barberini, his hand beckoning at fragments of a fissured globe. At the middle level, a man resembling Galileo, clad in a robe figured in geometric shapes, points with exuberance to the model of a dam which holds back the floodwaters of a river. Several others crowd around to look at the model. On the bottom level, three men, who could be mistaken equally for simple fishermen or for devils, hold a net positioned as if to catch whatever falls from above.*)

AN UNSEEN VOICE (*in hollow measured tones*): Behold the people is one, and they have all one language . . . and now nothing will be restrained from them which they have imagined to do. (*long pause*) Thus the first book of Holy Scripture, Genesis, the Book of Creation.

SCENE ONE

(In front of the curtain, seated on an austere cot to one side of a small illuminated area—a prison cell—is Giordano Bruno. He has been imprisoned on suspicion of heresy; his pantheism included, but went far beyond, his belief in the Copernican system. First dawn does not touch his face, whose contours, as the scene progresses, are gradually outlined but never become identifiable. Standing are Roberto Cardinal Bellarmine, Consultor of the Holy Office and Christendom's leading theologian, along with the Commissary-General of the Inquisition. Bellarmine extends his hand, offering the prisoner his ring to be kissed. Bruno remains immobile.)

BRUNO: Not once, in these seven dungeoned years, have I been diverted from instructing the Roman Church in the truths of Divine creation. Having endured this test of belief, I am sent the one mind gifted to understand.
BELLARMINE: You have endured your privation most nobly.
BRUNO: A blessing. You have freed me to explore the infinite contours of my Divinity.
BELLARMINE: Kneel, Giordano Bruno. Kneel and repent, so your spirit may ascend to heaven from that courtyard where the disembodying fire is prepared.
BRUNO: You come for murder.
BELLARMINE: For mercy.
BRUNO: Your mercy has too short a reach. Can you forgive the stars their infinity or pardon the earth its movement?
BELLARMINE: Your imagined universe is of no concern. Philosophy has no concern with God.
BRUNO: All His works contain Him. I see Him in every voiceless particle of the world.

BELLARMINE: Our three-personed God cannot survive such division. I no longer doubt the incurable fervor of your heresy.
BRUNO: You think me mad.
BELLARMINE: I hoped it. The Holy Father hoped it. Your admirers among the Fathers hoped it. But the interrogations of our most profound inquisitors have failed to find a disrupting flaw in the ordered clarity of your mind.
BRUNO: You think a momentary flame will undo what the armies of the Church could not loosen?
BELLARMINE: You have kindled them. False faith must be expelled.
BRUNO: By burning the believer? Are you so fearful?
BELLARMINE: Not fearful. Mortal. Our Lord might have accomplished it with a touch. We have been confined to natural devices.
BRUNO: Then why have you come? A cardinal has no special skills for fire.
BELLARMINE: For the salvation of your soul.
BRUNO: I offer that same glory to you—if you will join me?
BELLARMINE: Kneel, Giordano Bruno. Choose the penance of moments over an eternity of searing flesh.

(*Bruno does not stir. Bellarmine beckons. Two men enter, yank Bruno roughly to his feet, wrap him in the cloak of a condemned man, and lead him offstage.*)

BELLARMINE: A man of genius. In another office, I might have enjoyed his company.
COMMISSARY-GENERAL: His false prophecies challenged the faith.
BELLARMINE: False? Of course . . . false. If not, we have made a martyr. If so, we have burnt a heretic. (*shrugs his shoulders*) We have done as we considered we had to do. Judgment on our acts is now left to God . . . who will not hesitate to reveal it to us.

ACT ONE

SCENE TWO

(*To the left front of the stage is a wooden worktable, where Galileo Galilei and Marcantonio Mazzoleni, Galileo's assistant and instrument maker, are preparing an experiment.*

(*A professor of mathematics at the University of Padua, Galileo, in his mid-forties, has settled into the appearance he will retain for most of his life. He is a little above average height, his frame square-angled and well proportioned. Deep-set and lively eyes give his countenance a generally cheerful and pleasant aspect. The sanguine undertone of his fair complexion is complemented by red-hued abundant hair and a heavy beard which partly covers the white flaxen collar of his scholar's gown. Except for streaks of gray and a countenance made more grave by illness and ill fortune, the Galileo of seventy will look much like this obscure scholar who, in the prime of his powers, is standing, unaware, at the threshold of glory.*

(*On the table are six strips of wood, about two inches wide by one and a half inches thick—three precisely equal pairs of differing lengths between two and six feet. Along each strip is a concave depression whose rounded sides are highly polished; a small ball can roll easily along these concave channels without being obstructed by irregularities in the wood. There are also some wooden blocks, in pairs of exactly the same size. In a dish lie two round metal balls, and a polishing cloth is placed beside the dish. The initial impression of clutter yields to awareness that the objects must be essential to the particular "experiment" Galileo is performing. To the unknowing observer, Galileo's casual, rather ebullient manner and somewhat random conversation well might appear inconsistent with the meticulous precision of his hands as he manipulates and arranges these objects. By setting one end of a wooden strip on a wooden block he forms an inclined plane; by setting two identical strips on two identically sized blocks, he forms two such planes: their length is the same and they form identical angles* to the top of the table. *The planes are facing so that the bottom of one is perfectly fitted to the bottom of the other, permitting a ball to roll down one and up the other.*

(*Benedetto Castelli, a monk who is a young student of Galileo's, opens the door, sees the two men at work, and begins to withdraw, but not before Galileo notices him.*)

GALILEO: Castelli . . . come here. (*Castelli reenters and moves to Galileo's side.*) A young man, with strong pulse. Just what we need—eh, Mazzoleni?

(*Mazzoleni remains intent on setting up the ramps for the experiment.*)

GALILEO (*motions to Castelli*): The other side . . . stand there. (*Castelli walks around to the other side of the table, opposite Galileo.*) Place your finger on your wrist. (*Castelli does so.*) Can you feel the pulse?
CASTELLI: Yes.
GALILEO: Fortunately. At the instant of a pulsebeat, say "Now." I will release the ball. Count your pulsebeats until the ball reaches the bottom . . . here . . . at the intersection of the ramps.
CASTELLI (*concentrating intently*): Now!
GALILEO: Not yet.

(*Galileo and Mazzoleni lean over, carefully straightening and aligning the ramps. Satisfied, Galileo straightens, takes the ball gently between his thumb and forefinger, and holds it, with meticulous precision, just resting on the top edge of the ramp and looks to Castelli.*)

GALILEO: I await your pleasure.

(*Castelli looks up, inadvertently removing his finger from his wrist. As Galileo waits patiently, he looks down and fumbles for the pulse point.*)

CASTELLI: There, I have it . . . Now.

(*Galileo releases the ball, which accelerates down the ramp and begins to roll up the opposing incline, where Mazzoleni takes it.*)

CASTELLI: Seven.
GALILEO: Are you sure? We can try again.
CASTELLI: Seven. Exactly seven.

(*Galileo picks up a larger ball and resumes the ritual of polishing and examining the surface.*)

GALILEO: And this one, Castelli? How long? What is your guess.
CASTELLI: Four beats; maybe five.
GALILEO: Why?
CASTELLI: Heavier objects fall more quickly. It is well established.
GALILEO: Established? By whom?
CASTELLI: Aristotle.
GALILEO: You can read; that is established. (*He places the ball at the top of the ramp and looks expectantly toward Castelli.*)
CASTELLI: Now.

(*The ball rolls to the bottom and is picked off by Mazzoleni as it starts up the other side.*)

CASTELLI: There's something wrong. With my wrist, I mean.
GALILEO: The count.
CASTELLI: Six. Almost seven. I mean, I counted six, but I could feel another throb start just as it reached the bottom.
GALILEO: Close as our crude instruments will allow.
CASTELLI: But Aristotle—
GALILEO: Was wrong. Just think, Benedetto, you and I in this tiny room have just disproved the master of all philosophy, along with

two thousand years of cackling parrots. (*smiles at Castelli*) We call them scholars, Benedetto.

CASTELLI: Perhaps we . . . I . . . made some error.

GALILEO: Had it been otherwise, only one conclusion was possible. You would need a doctor for your pulse. The mathematics are precise. (*Suddenly absorbed, he paces thoughtfully along the table, not listening as Castelli begins to speak.*)

CASTELLI: The weight doesn't matter! But we are taught it is the nature of heavy objects to fall. It can't be . . . nothing inside the ball. (*triumphantly*) Or different objects would have different falls.

(*During Castelli's monologue, Galileo has picked up a ball.*)

GALILEO: Look, another problem, not so easy. (*He releases the ball and lets it roll to the bottom. As it starts to ascend the opposing ramp, Mazzoleni reaches over to intercept it, but Galileo holds up his hand.*) Don't touch it. (*The ball rolls up the opposing ramp, slowing until it stops and begins to roll back. Galileo, showing more excitement, picks up another ball and repeats the trial.*) It goes up. Why?

CASTELLI: It always does. It must . . . because . . .

GALILEO: We know there is an attraction toward the earth. But upward . . . there is no attraction.

CASTELLI: An arrow flies after it leaves the bow; a stone rises from the hurtling catapult.

GALILEO: Excellent, Benedetto. You have a fertile imagination. Find more examples. You may provide us with some new method: how to sum knowledge by adding ignorance to ignorance. (*Castelli, dismayed, falls silent. Galileo picks up still another ball.*) Watch closely. There is a clue. (*He repeats the trial, and looks at Castelli, who looks back quizzically.*) The length of the climb is the same as the distance of the descent. If the distances are the same, the forces must be the same.

CASTELLI: But we know only one force—attraction to the earth.
GALILEO: There is only one force. That is why the ball slows down as it rises.
CASTELLI: But that does not explain—
GALILEO: I know. (*Galileo repeats the trial a few more times, without observing closely, talking aloud but to himself.*) We must forget what we know. It blunts our power to reason.
CASTELLI: There is a work by—
GALILEO (*interrupting*): No book. No answer is known, so no authority exists. (*pauses*) One force, two motions—opposite and equal. (*pauses*) That is possible only if—(*He wheels toward Castelli.*) It must be!
CASTELLI: I can think of nothing.
GALILEO: Once an object is forced to move, it will keep moving, until another force interferes. In our case, both forces are the same.
CASTELLI: The arrow? . . . The catapult?
GALILEO: Propelled by bow or sling, arrested by resistance of air and attraction of the earth. It is the same. The forces are not the same. The principle is the same. (*He pauses, paces with increased excitement.*) And the conclusion. Immense! Surpassing imagination.
CASTELLI: Beyond mine.
GALILEO: If we are right . . . Suppose we should roll a ball along a surface—an imaginary surface . . . none could exist in nature . . . without friction, of indefinite length, every point of equal distance from the earth. How far would it roll?
CASTELLI: The calculation would take some time.
GALILEO: Forever! It would roll forever. The distance, infinite. The time, eternity. A law of motion. The governing law, the decree from which all other forms of motion are derived.
CASTELLI: Law? Decree? Of whose enactment?
GALILEO: Of God! Don't you see, Castelli, the law of motion must

be the decree of Him who created motion. It is a glimpse into the mind of God, who has granted us, this day, the power to know His works! . . . to share in the Mystery of Divine Creation.

(Galileo bows his head and crosses himself. Castelli and Mazzoleni do the same. The lights go down.)

Note to Scene Two

Galileo is demonstrating his discovery of the principle of inertia—although it was not named and fully described until later—which holds that a body maintains its state of rest or motion until acted upon by some external force. It is the seminal idea of post-Renaissance physics. In other words, a moving body will continue to move forever unless restrained by a force external to it. For earthly objects there is always some such force. Galileo came very close to a full understanding of this idea, which only came to completion in the work of Isaac Newton, born Christmas Day of the year Galileo died.

But the principle of inertia is not our greatest interest. We are witnessing not just a new scientific discovery but a new scientific method—and since science *is* method—it is the birth of science as we moderns understand it.

Up to now pure science had been a branch of philosophy. One arrived at certain basic principles through the power of intellect and observation, and then reasoned from those principles. Aristotle, for example, held that all bodies had a motion which was natural to them—e.g., that it was in the "nature" of earthly materials (stones, wood, fruit, etc.) to fall toward the center of the earth. It was in the "nature" of fire to go upward. From this, all sorts of conclusions were drawn—e.g., that heavier bodies would fall faster than light bodies. This also meant that a movement against the "natural" movement was "unnatural" and had to be attributed to some "violent" force. Once this force was removed, the body would return to its "natural" nonviolent motion. This made it hard to explain why an arrow or a thrown projectile continued on its "unnatural" course after it left the bow or the thrower's hand, and many elaborate explanations were offered—e.g., that the object's passage through the air created a vacuum which closed behind it and pressed it forward, or that something called impetus was impressed upon the object and kept it going.

It did not occur to the Aristotelians to test their theories of motion by what we would call experiment. From first principles, certain things followed. One could challenge the course of the reasoning but only by applying rules of logical rationality. The change that Galileo represents and helped to make consisted of two enormous shifts in the manner of describing and understanding the natural world.

First, Galileo thought that the "laws" or "rules" of nature were essentially mathematical. For instance, there was a law that bodies would persist in their state of motion were it not for restraining forces of gravity, friction, etc. This was true despite the fact one could not possibly free an actual earthly object from such external restraining forces. Nevertheless, the rule was true. Could we but measure exactly the amount of the restraining force, we could tell how rapidly the moving object would slow down or stop.

Thus, we were no longer investigating the "nature" of things but the mathematics of its behavior. Many qualities of an object which might be of most human interest—taste, color, smell, texture, use—were irrelevant. For science, the only significant difference between an apple and a stone was that of weight or mass or specific gravity. Galileo was driving science into a new kind of mathematical austerity, abstracted from the concern of humanists, astrologers, and theologians. And he was the first. Johannes Kepler was a greater astronomer than Galileo, but his work was motivated in part by the desire to demonstrate the musical harmony of the heavens. There is no such mysticism in Galileo's work. His writings speak directly to the modern mind.

Second, Galileo was the first to combine science and technology. There had been many important technological advances during the Middle Ages, but they were not thought to have anything to do with science. True, mathematicians and astronomers were often expected to advise on building fortifications or casting horoscopes, but this was because the study of "science" was not thought significant enough to exempt them from making more practical contributions.

Galileo was both inventor and theorist, and he used each talent to supplement the other. He made new instruments, not only for immediate practical uses but also to provide fresh observations for scientific theory. Out of this evolved the experimental method—an interplay of abstract theory and tangible demonstration. One devised experiments to prove or refine a theory which was already constructed. Unless this were the purpose the experiments would make no sense—why should one roll balls down planes at all? But the experiments could also yield results that might lead one to modify, refine, or even discard the theory, as many of Galileo's experiments disproved certain aspects of Aristotle's physics.

We are, therefore, observing the principal architect of scientific ideology—that system of beliefs which rules the world. This was far more important than any of his discoveries through the telescope.

SCENE THREE

(*A Vatican chamber. Pope Paul V is seated at the head of a table. Philip, King of Spain, enters, carrying a large scroll. He is accompanied by King Ferdinand of Bohemia. They sit, one on each side of the Pope.*)

POPE: Does Matthias live?
PHILIP: Barely.
POPE (*crosses himself and bends his head*): May merciful Christ grant swift recovery to the Holy Roman Emperor.
PHILIP: He will die.

POPE: We shall prepare masses for the salvation of his soul.
PHILIP: That is your office, Your Holiness. As King of Spain, I must prepare the Empire against the turmoil of his passing.
POPE: Will you seek the throne?
PHILIP: Not I. My cousin Ferdinand of Bohemia (*indicating*) will succeed. With your blessing, Your Holiness.
POPE (*to Ferdinand*): Your intention?
FERDINAND: To scourge the Lutheran heresy from the face of Europe and restore the universal church.
POPE: Do you have such strength?
FERDINAND: Not alone.
POPE (*to Philip*): Will you commit your armies to this most dangerous crusade?
PHILIP: With your help.
POPE: We shall offer continual prayers for your success.
PHILIP: A great comfort, Your Holiness. But I had something more secular in mind.
POPE: The papal armies are small. Is it gold?
PHILIP: Our treasuries overflow with Peruvian gold. (*He unscrolls and holds up the map of Europe that he has brought in.*) Here, the Lutheran kingdoms, firmly in control of all Northern Europe. The Spanish Netherlands (*pointing*) in revolt against my kingly rule.
POPE: I am well instructed in geography.
PHILIP: I must bring my power from here (*indicating*) to here, subdue the revolt of the Netherlands, and join with Ferdinand's imperial forces to march on northern Germany.
POPE: A wonderful plan, if your generals could fly the mountains of the Pyrenees.
PHILIP: There is another way.
POPE: Through Italy!
PHILIP (*pointing*): East, across Italy, then northward along the border of France.
POPE: France will never agree.

FERDINAND: Catholic France will not be disturbed.
PHILIP: Europe has been divided for a century. Every unchallenged year roots the Protestant heresy more firmly in the soil of Europe. Can you, Christ's own vicar, let this moment pass?
POPE: What would you have me do?
PHILIP: Guarantee our peaceful intentions to your Italy and to Catholic France.
POPE: With words that I lack power to enforce. I do have one weapon. And I will use it. We command you, Philip of Spain, and you, Ferdinand of Bohemia, to restrain your forces from attack against any Catholic kingdom. Should you disobey, we will decree you severed from the Church of Christ, declared most odious heretics, and consigned to eternal damnation.
PHILIP: You will have no cause, Your Holiness.
FERDINAND: We will end heresy, not embrace it.
POPE: I will convey my intentions and my sanctions to our ambassador in France. (*almost pleadingly*) You can master your souls. Can you master your armies?
PHILIP: You will have cause to rejoice in our triumph.
POPE: May almighty God have it so.

(*All rise. Pope Paul silently blesses them and leaves.*)

FERDINAND: He fears us. Without cause.
PHILIP: We will command the greatest army in Christendom.
FERDINAND: In his service. My sole design is to restore the Catholic empire.
PHILIP: And your destiny.
FERDINAND: We will shed no Catholic blood. I will risk no transgression, for pious fear of the Holy Father's most terrible power.
PHILIP: Over our souls. He has no power over the soul of a cannon. He cannot excommunicate a cannon.

SCENE FOUR

(*The study of the Papal Nuncio to France, Maffeo Cardinal Barberini, in his official residence, located on the fringes of Paris. Although luxurious to modern eyes, the room and the home which contains it are modest, almost spare, by the standards of the Cardinal's native Italy. A large elaborately carved desk of Circassian walnut faces out across the room from the wall stage left. Behind it, drawn curtains obscure Venetian glass doors which open to a small colonnade leading to a garden. On each side of the curtains and along the wall to the right of the desk are shelves filled with elaborately bound books. On the left wall is a painting of the adolescent Louis XIII seated on a throne constructed for a more mature and capacious frame; standing beside him, bending in whispered conversation, is the Chancellor and de facto ruler of France: Cardinal Richelieu. Under the tapestry on the right wall is a wide fireplace, whose smoldering logs are virtually consumed. On the desk, books, manuscripts, and papers are arranged so as to suggest a calculated, if idiosyncratic, order.*

(*Two workmen are hanging a large painting on the wall across from the Cardinal's desk. The work is done in a manner that combines Renaissance realism with spiritual allegory, hinting at the decadence which has already infected the art of the times. A suspended figure of Countess Matilda of Tuscany hovers with outspread arms over her mountaintop castle at Canossa. Her armies are not depicted, but the viewer would know they stand ready to protect the Pope if Emperor Henry IV should defy papal authority. The castle itself is painted in careful proportion to the mountain, as are the more distant figures who stand at the foot of the snow-covered pathway to the castle—Henry IV in the white garb of a penitent, followed by a handful of attendants. The painting starts to slip from the hand of the First Workman, who is trying to lift one side of its heavy frame. He struggles to maintain his grip.*)

First Workman (*with loud urgency*): Set it down!

(*The Second Workman lowers his side, until the painting is on the floor, resting against the wall.*)

First Workman (*blows on his hands to warm them*): They are as cold as the Emperor's toes. (*He points to the figure of Henry IV standing in the snow.*) Must my fingers do the same penitence to a cardinal as he to a pope? Guiltless fingers. (*He pauses, caresses the air as if his hand remembered the contours of a woman's breast.*) Well, perhaps not completely. Still, given fair judgment, their good works would outweigh their transgressions.
Second Workman: Not from choice.
First Workman: A man must work. That necessity begets virtue only proves His special concern for the salvation of the poor. (*crossing himself*) Surely a prince of His Church knows that cold workmen have clumsy hands. (*gestures toward the smoldering fire*)
Second Workman (*puts his finger to his lips*): The Cardinal has heavier concerns than the comfort of common carpenters.
First Workman (*deliberately raising his voice*): Barberini? Why, the eminence he stands upon was crafted by a Carpenter. The Pope of Rome is servant to that same Carpenter. If Our Lord chose to labor with wood, surely His priests might find a log or two for our fire.
Second Workman (*trying to silence him*): Let your blasphemy be overheard, and you may have more fire than you need.
First Workman: Blasphemy! Impossible! What is blasphemy but a disorder of men who imagine themselves the hammer and not the nail? (*beats his breast, striking a heroic pose*) I know myself a contemptible sinner, conceived in bodily sin, encased in sinful flesh. (*He throws himself upon his knees, looks at colleague, and instantly*

flattens his voice to the monotone precision of pure reason.) Blaspheme, I cannot. I am too humble.

SECOND WORKMAN: Lift your side. The Cardinal will be here any moment.

FIRST WORKMAN: Should the Cardinal appear, I would kneel to kiss his ring . . . kneel to his office, mind you, not the man. So, too, I ask for warmth in the name of my carpenter's trade, not for myself. For myself, not a kindling stick. (*He grips the frame as if to lift it, stops, stands erect blowing on his hands, then moves toward the fireplace with outstretched hands, sees that the fire is almost out, and turns back to the painting.*) Not even a flame.

SECOND WORKMAN: Your ravings may bring you warmth enough. You might yet become the Bruno of Paris.

FIRST WORKMAN: Bruno?

SECOND WORKMAN: Bruno is known everywhere in Europe, and yesterday became more famous still.

FIRST WORKMAN: And what great honor did he receive yesterday?

SECOND WORKMAN: He was burned at the stake.

FIRST WORKMAN: Truly a rare recognition. (*pauses*) This Bruno . . . he was not a carpenter?

SECOND WORKMAN: No, a heretic.

FIRST WORKMAN (*brightening visibly*): Good. I did not think they had begun to burn carpenters.

SECOND WORKMAN: Why? Cannot a carpenter be a heretic?

FIRST WORKMAN: We lack the genius to be heretics. The dullest and most ignorant may transgress the commands of God, but cannot debate them; sinners, not heretics. We will not burn.

SECOND WORKMAN: Then we are safe?

FIRST WORKMAN: From injustice.

SECOND WORKMAN: The Church is just.

FIRST WORKMAN: But also powerful. And no one is safe from power.

SECOND WORKMAN: You contradict yourself.
FIRST WORKMAN: Safe and not safe. Justice is Divine; eternity will correct the balance. Power is mortal; the possibility of correction perishes with its custodians.
SECOND WORKMAN: Your own correction may be very close if this picture is not quickly hung.
FIRST WORKMAN: If my hands were as warm as my tongue, they would perform as skillfully.
SECOND WORKMAN: Then put them in your mouth.
FIRST WORKMAN: A man of genius . . . practical genius. (*He puts fingers in his mouth, and continues to talk, his words garbled.*) My own fire . . . if . . . too stingy . . . a man of duty.

(*At this moment the door to the study opens and Cardinal Barberini enters, accompanied by Monsignor Ciampoli. Maffeo Cardinal Barberini is about forty, tall, with a large muscular frame, and olive complexion. His broad forehead and deep-set blue eyes give the impression of abundant energy, and he has a manner of intense observation whose swiftness of assimilation often makes him appear to combine restlessness with his formidable intelligence. Barberini wears his mustache fairly long and, in the fashion of the time, curled slightly upward at each end; his beard is of moderate length and squarely cut. With the exception of grayed hair and some distention of the cheeks, he will look much the same at seventy, although the elements of his temperament will be differently proportioned.*

(*The Cardinal's scholarly and artistic interests, although genuine, have not diluted his immense practical abilities, which, coupled with his self-confidence and an extraordinary capacity for long hours of work, have allowed him to make a rapid passage through the treacherous currents of ecclesiastical power. Having received the purple at the relatively early age of thirty-eight, he is now entrusted with a position of great importance to the welfare of the Church. His indefatigable dedication is, however, relieved by a sometimes sardonic hu-*

mor, a love of poetry, and an appreciative delight in men of wit and talent; an occasional lapse of control—a sudden anger, a transient revelation of some obsessive vision—hints at an element of passion unusual, even inappropriate, for a successful man of affairs.

(*His colleague, Monsignor Giovanni Ciampoli, is dressed in the simple gray habit of a monk. The cowl is laid back across his shoulders, exposing thick black hair surmounting a slightly rounded face which radiates the somewhat muted vitality appropriate for a man of both energy and learning. He is about the same age as Cardinal Barberini, and has been a close friend, colleague, and assistant since they met while students at the University of Pisa.*

Ciampoli is carrying a large white envelope fastened by a seal of red wax. The Cardinal gives a quick, slightly surprised glance at the First Workman, who, in some confusion, tries simultaneously to pull his fingers out of his mouth, to bend as if to lift the frame, and to bow toward the Cardinal.)

FIRST WORKMAN: Most illustrious.
SECOND WORKMAN: Most Reverend.

(*While speaking these customary forms of address, both men kneel. Barely breaking his customary rapid stride, Cardinal Barberini extends his hand to allow the men to kiss his ring and continues toward the desk, glancing toward the fireplace.*)

BARBERINI (*without looking back, in a tone more of comment than of command*): We need more wood.

(*The First Workman smiles rather smugly at his colleague and blows once more on his hands as they both turn to their work. Ciampoli walks back to the door and speaks briefly to a priest-attendant standing outside. The words are inaudible to the audience. While the scene continues, the priest will bring in an armful of logs, place three of* them on the fire, deposit the rest in a large brass container beside the fireplace, and leave, carefully closing the door behind him.

(*The Cardinal continues toward his desk and sits down. Ciampoli walks to the shelves behind the desk, where he begins looking for a book.*)

BARBERINI (*glancing toward the workmen*): Our Italian blood is too thin for your French winters.

(*The First Workman smiles and nods. Barberini begins writing something, then looks at Ciampoli, who is still holding the envelope.*)

BARBERINI: From Rome?
CIAMPOLI: And marked urgent. (*He hands the envelope to Barberini, who tears it open and reads as Ciampoli begins to look at a book.*)
BARBERINI: The Holy Roman Emperor is dead.

(*Ciampoli crosses himself. Barberini, prompted by the gesture, rises and does the same.*)

CIAMPOLI: May his soul find peace in the bosom of the Lord.
BARBERINI: As it will shatter the peace of the kingdom he leaves behind.
CIAMPOLI: The election will be furiously contested.
BARBERINI: It is already decided.
CIAMPOLI: Who?
BARBERINI: A Hapsburg . . . a poor Hapsburg, but still, a Hapsburg: Ferdinand of Bohemia—"hammer of the heretics."
CIAMPOLI: And the price?
BARBERINI: The Holy Father will allow Ferdinand's cousin Spain free transit through the Italian passes. Joined by Germans he will

march northward to overthrow the Lutheran kingdoms of northern Germany.

CIAMPOLI: Along the borders of France?

BARBERINI: Rome has required most solemn guarantees. And I am assigned to persuade Richelieu to stake his kingdom on the word of a Spaniard.

CIAMPOLI: Can the Lutheran heresy be toppled?

BARBERINI: Perhaps.

CIAMPOLI: Most bloodily?

BARBERINI: Of ferocity unknown since Caesar's legions. (*He picks up a large, black leather-bound Bible from his desk and exhibits it to Ciampoli.*) The faith of Christ. How could we have failed him so?

CIAMPOLI: You are too harsh. The Holy Office did not draft the dogmas of Luther, or dispatch the devil to tickle the lusts of a libertine English king.

BARBERINI (*shaking the Bible*): Yet . . . in here . . . He permits no such comforting justification. Weakness is no excuse; adversity contains no pardon; ignorance does not justify. Obedience is all.

CIAMPOLI: You might command me to leap from this rooftop and fly to the center of Paris. I could jump, but I am unlikely to reach Paris.

BARBERINI: How do you know, Giovanni? You are a man of surprising gifts. Imagine the confusion at court when you soar through the windows of Versailles. The first Italian angel. You must do it. For the honor of Italy.

CIAMPOLI: It would be even more memorable if we went together.

BARBERINI: True. (*He glances toward the window.*) But it is almost night, and we might lose our way. Another time.

(*Outside can be heard the faint sounds of approaching hoofbeats.*)

BARBERINI: As I expected. The keenest eyes in Europe will have read most ominous import in this news.

CIAMPOLI: Shall I turn him back?
BARBERINI: You cannot. Not this man. His fierce alarm would rupture our thin gates.

(*There are three sharp and peremptory raps on the door. Barberini looks up, shows a momentary anger, quickly masked. He glances at Ciampoli, who goes toward the door, but it swings open before he can reach it, and an agitated Cardinal Richelieu enters the room, past the restraining gesture of the priest who has conducted him to the study.*

(*Armand du Plessis, Duc de Richelieu, made cardinal at the age of thirty-eight, King Louis XIII's Chief Minister at forty, is the de facto ruler of France and will remain so until his death. In less than two cacophonous decades he was to lead, indeed will, France across the boundary from being a feeble coalition of medieval fiefdoms to becoming the nation whose fused obedience would permit the King's successor, Louis XIV, to preside over what was to be called the Golden Age of France.*

(*These years of transforming labor still lay ahead of the man who, without slowing his entrance, has already begun to discard the drab, brown traveling cloak which protects his hued robes of ecclesiastical office, first brushing back the hood that conceals his red biretta. Although equal in height to his contemporary, Richelieu, unlike the robust Barberini, is thin to the point of frailty; his sharp-peaked features and concave cheeks are accentuated by a short beard of acute triangular cut. The tight angularity of his face does not diminish the impression of insistent passion fueled by great energies. Only the unnaturally condensed brilliance of his eyes, cold as the evening star, betrays the nimble premeditations of a rare observing power whose judgments are as detached from his own emotions and behavior as from those of others. He is, that is, a romantic idealist endowed with extraordinary practical skills, a blend characteristic of murderous tyrants, heroic leaders, and Greek gods. Had he been born a Medici, Machiavelli would have been a prophet.*

(*A few steps into the room, Richelieu halts abruptly, looks sternly toward the workmen, who, having completed their task, quickly leave, and then turns to the desk where Cardinal Barberini is rising to greet him. Before Barberini is fully erect, Richelieu turns back to the painting.*)

RICHELIEU (*pointing at the white garbed figure at the foot of the mountain*): Ah, Canossa! A great moment for the Church. There he is! The Emperor of all Europe, heir to insolent Charlemagne —poor little Henry, his regal toes bound to icy penance in the snow, until Pope Gregory (*points to castle*) finishes his meal and consents to the salvation of his immortal soul.

BARBERINI: An apostate king submits to the Church of Christ. The illustration is a personal favorite. But if you are here to intervene, you come six centuries too late.

RICHELIEU: Strange, is it not, that he did not fear the flames of hell (*pointing to the figure of Countess Matilda*) until the sainted Countess Matilda reinforced the edicts of Gregory with the armies of Italy. (*crosses himself*) The mysteries of the Almighty are infinite. (*He pauses, turns abruptly, finger pointed at Barberini.*) Is this what you have in mind for the King of France?

BARBERINI (*still calm, but somewhat abruptly, making an effort to mask his rising anger*): My mind, as the Chancellor knows, contains no purpose except the church, which designs solely to heal the Lutheran plague which fevers all of Northern Europe.

RICHELIEU (*suddenly very cold*): How?

BARBERINI (*intervening in a soothing tone*): That is in the hands of God.

RICHELIEU (*muttering, as if to himself*): Safer hands for France. (*His voice rises, becomes accusatorial. He turns to the picture, speaking with a strident, almost hysterical insistence.*) There! (*points at the figure of Henry IV*) King Louis is to be spared only the snow. His Canossa is to be Madrid. His Matilda, Philip of Spain. Inform your Rome that he will not make so mild a journey. Tell your Spain to stable its horses and prepare its fleet, for we will flood their path with rivers of blood too broad for armies; pious Catholic blood, enough to make all Castile one brimmed chalice for this unholy sacrament.

BARBERINI (*patiently*): As usual, my Lord Chancellor, your mind outleaps our ordinary understanding.

RICHELIEU: Admirable. How admirably you play the innocent. You should have been a politician. Rome, it seems, has chosen to envenom the arrows of most dangerous ambition. It must have been prayer, pious contemplation, perhaps even a glint, a perceptible whiff, of immortal will, for no feeble human intellect, no mortal conclave, could have wondrously concluded to invite to table companions of such insatiable greed that—their appetites once awakened—they might make a final course of their kindly hosts: St. Peter's, Castel Gandolfo, the Papal States, and all the caped and crowned rulers of God's earthly court.

BARBERINI: You fear Ferdinand?

RICHELIEU: No more than you. Which is not all . . . A barbarian, an animal trained to piety, a sapless club to enforce another's will—a German! Admittedly, the best kind of German—a German without power. He is no enemy. He is an enemy's costume. He is the mask of Spanish might.

BARBERINI: And a most obedient Catholic.

RICHELIEU: This obedient Ferdinand. This Catholic Ferdinand. This new Emperor of half the world, is to place Spanish armies in your Italy and on the borders of France. All this with the blessings of ignorant, blind, suicidal Rome.

BARBERINI: If Christ must be fulfilled by the sword, his servants must not fear its use.

RICHELIEU: You have a truly modern mind. Our more primitive ancestors confined their crusades to Turks. You have discovered we must also make war on fellow worshippers.

BARBERINI: Enemies to the faith.

RICHELIEU: Christians! Is the Lutheran not a Christian? Nor the Englishman?
BARBERINI: Their Christianity is their horror. Those who have never known Christ are beyond the faith. Those who know, yet deny the Church, mutilate Christ's own body.
RICHELIEU: Softly, my friend. Like you, I am obedient to the one true Catholic faith.
BARBERINI: Truth! Who speaks of truth? Who dares? Your Catholic faith, Lord Chancellor, is unquestioned. But you are mistaken to claim it the one true faith. It is the only possible faith. The Church is our Creator's act of mercy. To deny Rome is to deny His gift. Those who deny His gift, reject Him. Those who allow denial, betray Him.
RICHELIEU: And for this miraculous reconciliation, the Vicar of Christ on earth—the present Vicar—will, reluctantly but dutifully, sacrifice his most obedient, most loyal, and most Catholic France.
BARBERINI: Spanish power, if it comes, need only be feared by heretic princes.
RICHELIEU: The enmity between Spain and France is older than living memory. Almost every Spanish defeat has had a French hand, and every Spanish king has tried to reduce defiant France. Despite Spain's swelling power, it has failed. For Almighty God, in His justice, has placed a wall of high-peaked rock between them and fruitful France. But even God's frontiers must be guarded by men. Do you believe your devious Spaniards will not be drawn to the beguiling fragrance of France, which will assault their every mile toward the throned and frozen north?
BARBERINI: You underestimate the strength of France.
RICHELIEU: The strength of France! There is no France. A dozen provinces held by rebellious dukes, thirty cities fortified under Huguenot rule. The name of King Louis is honored everywhere; the arms of Louis scarcely reach beyond the bridges of Paris. (*pauses,*

his tone more subdued) I have not come to lament. You may report a great success. France will not take the field. (*pause*) I lack the strength to oppose.

BARBERINI: In return?

RICHELIEU: What I have already found: an ally. (*He reaches for his cloak and turns toward the door.*)

BARBERINI: Does the Chancellor of France tire so quickly?

RICHELIEU (*interrupting*): You are officer to a pope, I to a king. But we are not functionaries, you and I. You serve a dream, a vision out of the past. I serve fields and cities and the young ruler of a kingdom yet to come! The times have chanced to mate us—each to the other's purpose.

BARBERINI: Do you think to breed the elephant with the eagle?

RICHELIEU: I mean nothing unnatural. But the elephant's back can bear a weary eagle, and a farseeing eagle can guide the forested elephant. I know the decisions are not yours to make. In Rome I wish you only to exercise your influence toward the protection of France.

BARBERINI: Shall we fear a conquering Catholic cross?

RICHELIEU (*his voice rising, loud but controlled*): A Catholic cross, but the cross of the Hapsburgs, not that of Rome. Should it lead their armies to the icy Baltic—may God forbid it—all Europe will be Catholic. But its conqueror will be Caesar. Do you think this new swollen Caesar will lay his conquests at the feet of the Holy Father? That would be a Caesar and, more than Caesar, a saint. Europe has room for a pope and many kings. The whole world is not large enough to contain a pope and one, single king. (*There is no response. Richelieu's words seem silently suspended between the Chancellor and Barberini. After a pause he continues.*) Surely you, Barberini, are wise enough to know the folly of this enterprise.

BARBERINI: My only wisdom is in obedience.

RICHELIEU: You obey, but you also think. I seek a place in the world. You would heal it. You cannot heal by playing physician to the mighty. It is His body which bleeds, Barberini, and new wounds open faster than you can dam the old. On this cankered globe, steel alone can halt descending steel. The sword of France is made of steel; the blades of France will be a shield for Christ —knowing that those who menace you would smother striving France.

I no longer know *how* Rome thinks. Or *if* Rome thinks. But surely *you* understand that the power of France is bound to the protection of Rome—not by loyalty or by faith—but by the strongest of all worldly bonds: by survival, by *our . . . sovereign . . . life*. (*He pauses. There is no response from his immobile auditors.*) Our union is thus sealed by necessity, which binds, they say, Almighty God Himself.

BARBERINI (*with soft intensity*): I wish you well, my friend.
RICHELIEU (*turning from the embrace*): I know. I know you do. (*The lights have gradually been concentrated on the Chancellor until now he seems almost alone on the stage. He stands calmly in the doorway, his voice becoming softer and more intimate.*) I saw you first when you presented your credentials, standing before the throne of young Louis. Even I, the most contingent of men, hardly dare the conjecture that I may next look upon you from bended knees. You would certainly look the part . . . in a few years . . . with a little more gray in your beard. We shall miss you in Paris. But you should leave. Since the Ascension of Our Lord, destiny has never gone in search of men. (*He departs, and the door closes behind him.*)

SCENE FIVE

(Barberini resumes his seat, studying his manuscript. Ciampoli remains standing, still looking toward the closed door.)

BARBERINI *(looking up)*: Have you ever seen a Spanish sword? *(picks up a metal letter opener)* A most ingenious weapon. *(runs his finger along it)* Unlike ours, ground on both its sides: a doubled blade which looks most keenly toward both victim and companion, dangerous to all but the man who holds it. *(He grasps the opener with a fierce, sudden movement, holding it up, at the same time reducing his voice to a low flat tone.)* Which is why the attacking Spanish infantry spreads its ranks. It is the highest proof of Spanish genius.

CIAMPOLI: If the Catholic Church must fear Catholic armies, there must be no war.

BARBERINI: There is no other way.

CIAMPOLI: Is this Protestant doctrine so monstrous?

BARBERINI: More than a doctrine. Worse than a heresy. This Lutheran brew seduces each man to believe he is his own church of Christ. Around him, the stars will swing and the spheres of heaven revolve. Within him is inscribed Christ's chart toward the soul's own kingdom. The labors of our Holy Fathers, unnecessary; the wisdom of the saints, unnecessary; the teachings of Peter's heirs, unnecessary. Yet if God's authority on earth is not granted to His Church, then it is shared by every man. Where all can claim authority, there is no authority for all. Truth is merely the wish of each. Yet only God's will can be the truth. Now, Giovanni, now do you see how powerful a liquor is brewed—that makes all men Gods. How swiftly it must transform them into contending beasts!

CIAMPOLI: The physic which can purge our limbs may poison the heart.

BARBERINI: In the hands of a clumsy surgeon.
CIAMPOLI: The Church is a surgeon.
BARBERINI: True.
CIAMPOLI: And also patient to the surgeon.
BARBERINI: The Church is many things.
CIAMPOLI: And many people. Who then shall guide the knife?
BARBERINI: The Holy Father. He is sovereign. (*He falls silent, looks down at papers on his desk, although one cannot be sure whether he is reading or absorbed in thought. Ciampoli stares toward his bent head. Barberini slowly lifts his head and turns until he is facing Ciampoli.*) Is it a sin to want the throne? Is it, Giovanni? And to seek it by act, not by supplicating prayer?
CIAMPOLI: God chose Peter and left the burden of succession to men. One does not pray to other men.
BARBERINI: No. They must be seduced.
CIAMPOLI: There is no other way. But God's grace accompanies the terrible burden of His freedom.
BARBERINI: Freedom! Free to praise the wisdom of senile clerics. Free to laugh at the witless gibes of princes. Free for hypocrisy, free for deception, free to voice outright lies. Is it so required? (*pauses*) Is it wrong to pursue that which is His to grant?
CIAMPOLI: Not if He guides your search.
BARBERINI: And how will I know?
CIAMPOLI: If you are wrong . . . you forfeit the salvation of your soul.
BARBERINI: And even if I am right?
CIAMPOLI: Even so. Should that sacrifice be required of you?
BARBERINI: To become pope, and then to merit damnation. That is irony enough for both of us. I assume, my dear Giovanni, that my closest accomplice in this world will share my destination in the next. (*begins to smile*) Remember my first sermon? All the great families were there. The Bishop of Florence was himself the first

to praise me. Every heartbeat seemed the tread of advancing glory . . . until you corrected my reference to Aquinas—in a discreet whisper, naturally. I had missed the point entirely.

CIAMPOLI: It was a triumph.

BARBERINI: It was all wrong. I had many admirers that day but only one friend. It is still the same.

CIAMPOLI: Should your ascent continue, it is said that men who arrive at great heights pass beyond the claims of friendship.

BARBERINI: It is they who need them most. Can advancing ambition trace a path through the swarm of flattery and slander without one honest voice, one judgment without motive, one witness without judgment? The cost of such a triumph would be love of self—an earthly madness and a mortal sin. But the love of friends needs no reason. Are we not both poets?

CIAMPOLI: We both write poetry.

BARBERINI: Alone, we write poetry. Together, we are poets. As we are unlikely to find a third candidate for our small academy, artistic necessity keeps us friends. (*Ciampoli walks over toward the fireplace and stands pensively before the flames.*) Do you see Europe burning?

CIAMPOLI: Not all heresy. Just one heretic.

BARBERINI: Bruno? He was justly burned; a necessity.

CIAMPOLI: Yet there were fragments of truth in Bruno's heresy.

BARBERINI: Truth. You sound like Richelieu. Truth is a modern prejudice. There is the message and the church of Christ. That is a truth. (*picks up pen and drops it to the desk*) The pen falls. Also a truth.

CIAMPOLI: Unless you have mastered magic.

BARBERINI: Two truths. But not the same. One is the word of God; the other merely observation. He is truth. We are merely opinion.

CIAMPOLI: Would you abandon philosophy?

BARBERINI: Of course not. Nor art. Nor music. A church of this world must display the seductive glories of this world.

CIAMPOLI: It is a mistake to make martyrs. Bruno could have been left to the dungeon.
BARBERINI: In other times, perhaps. But when rebellion is in the air, the voice of unrebuked heresy can raise armies. (*He begins to rise from his desk, slowly, with a touch of weariness, and looks toward the garden beyond the chamber doors.*) Does the garden have a moon?

(*Ciampoli walks to the curtained glass doors behind the Cardinal and pushes them open. At first the trees and bushes seem only dark shapes against the deep night blue of the sky. Gradually, as our pupils open to the night, a few of the brightest stars appear, then a multitude. In that part of the sky just beyond the garden wall, and slightly to the right, there is a small streak of light, as if some celestial artist, his concentration wearied by the exacting demands of his precisely patterned subject, had inadvertently smeared the canvas with somewhat frayed and whitened brush. Ciampoli stands immobile, staring toward the sky.*)

BARBERINI: A moon. You'll know it. A large white disk, quite bright, widely celebrated for its occasional evening displays.
CIAMPOLI: No moon . . . but something marvelous! A comet. There is a comet. (*Barberini gets up from his desk and goes to stand beside Ciampoli. He scans the night sky, obviously searching. Ciampoli points at the streak of light.*) There. (*Barberini leans toward Ciampoli, sights along the directing finger, then stands apart, his eyes fixed with unusual intensity on the thin, imprecise slash of light.*)
BARBERINI: Do you suppose it can be seen in Rome?
CIAMPOLI (*excitedly*): In Rome, and Prague, perhaps even in savage America.
BARBERINI: Is it not said that a comet is the courser of heaven; that, once unbuckled, thrones expel their kings, the feathered pillow stops the breath of infant heirs, hollow famine pursues the

gluttonous plague, kingdoms fall one upon the other, and the map of the great globe itself is fissured?
CIAMPOLI: That is the general superstition, absent the lyrical gilding which is your own endowment.
BARBERINI: I share your skepticism.
CIAMPOLI: The Bible teaches that the heavens will manifest the dread terror of His justice when He returns. Yet that small, dim line (*pointing*) could not even light our garden path. Scarcely an illumination equal to momentous prophecy.
BARBERINI: Comets are not often seen. Are they stars? But stars do not move.
CIAMPOLI: Only as a whole, not in relation to one another. So Aristotle tells us.
BARBERINI: You agree?
CIAMPOLI: The Church agrees. (*pauses*) A friend of mine has written that comets are earthly vapors made luminous by the sun. He is a professor employed by the Venetian Republic . . . at the University in Padua.
BARBERINI: A professor of comets. The commerce of Venice must be prospering.
CIAMPOLI: No. Much more. A philosopher of nature. A man of extraordinary gifts. Do we go to Venice? You will meet.
BARBERINI: To Venice? Yes, we shall stop in Venice on the way.
CIAMPOLI: To where?
BARBERINI (*musingly*): As a child, I can remember waking from a vision of terror . . . tumbling from bed to the escape of my mother's arms.
CIAMPOLI: Were you very young?
BARBERINI: Twelve, a little more . . . the first time. But it came again . . . the same dream . . . once, perhaps twice a year. I was on a ship for Rome, as a prisoner, I think. For though I was not bound, two hugely armored soldiers stood watch beside me. Then

without warning the seas engorged our ship and flung it on an island of stone from which there was no escape.
CIAMPOLI: Has this dream stayed with you?
BARBERINI: Not since at sixteen I went to live with my uncle, an official of the Roman Curia . . . never since then . . . until last night. It was the same dream, but a different ending. Still a child, I climbed a high rock; standing there, I commanded the crew and all the soldiers to follow me to Rome; they need not fear, our safe passage had been assured by an angel of God.
CIAMPOLI: So we go to Rome.
BARBERINI: Not in obedience to a dream. That would be sacrilege. (*He brightens, his voice rising with enthusiasm.*) There is to be a war. We would not miss the war.
CIAMPOLI: There is no war in Rome.
BARBERINI: Not *in* Rome, *for* Rome. All the world will fight for Rome. We are not made to be spectators, you and I. We must be there, Giovanni. We belong there.

SCENE SIX

(*Padua, a city of the Venetian Republic, site of the most prestigious university in Europe. We are in a large room that constitutes the entire second floor of Galileo's modest home and serves as a combined workshop, kitchen, and dining space for Galileo; his mistress, Marina Gamba; his daughter, Maria Celeste, who had become a nun some time before; and his instrument maker, Mazzoleni. On the eastern wall, at the rear of the stage, three large windows of Venetian glass have been opened to the afternoon sun. They guide the eye across twenty-four miles of gentle, vined hills to Venice, which, from a distance,* appears as a red-hued cluster of buildings divided by narrow blue veins and abruptly bordered by the blue-tinted Adriatic.

(*Galileo is seated at a large roughly finished wood dining table. He is dressed in almost ostentatious simplicity in contrast to the fashionable multihued, tight-fitting lace bloomers, and stockings worn by the Venetian Senators who are about to enter.*

(*Gioan [Giovanni] Francesco Sagredo, an eccentric and wealthy Venetian patrician and a close friend, stands beside Galileo. Another of Galileo's friends, Filippo Salviatti, a noble of Florence, is at the window amiably helping to adjust and align a telescope [called a "spyglass" or "eye reed" until named "telescope" at a meeting of the Lyncean Academy in Rome a year or two later. Galileo always referred to this particular telescope as "Old Discoverer"].*

(*Sister Maria Celeste is seated behind her father, playing softly, almost imperceptibly, on a lute, occasionally adding her voice to the thrummed strings. Across the table from Galileo, Mazzoleni, wearing his workman's apron, is wholly concentrated on the work of meticulously polishing a small convex lens.*)

SAGREDO: They are coming.
GALILEO: It is ready.
SAGREDO: You need only conceal your contempt. Salviatti and I will do the rest.
GALILEO: I have no contempt for their wealth. I envy it. As for their ideas, they have none.
SAGREDO: The Senators of Venice confine their speculations to goods. They will leave the world to you.
GALILEO: Which they value far less than the things it contains, unless they think poverty a goad to philosophy.
SAGREDO: Teachers are abundant, so their services are cheap. An elementary rule of commerce. But this new invention of yours is a rarity.
GALILEO: The spyglass? Yes, now I have something to sell.

(*Several Venetian Senators enter, nod gravely to Galileo, greet Sagredo warmly, and are led to the center window by Salviatti, where they somewhat excitedly take turns looking through a long wooden tube bound in heavy parchment, supported on a wooden stand, and pointed toward Venice. Of varying age, most of the Venetian nobles are slender, fair, and with short haircuts—characteristics that distinguish them from most other inhabitants of the Italian peninsula.*)

SAGREDO (*aside to Galileo*): Let us handle them. And, if possible, smile.
GALILEO (*with a mock nod*): Your most obedient servant.

(*The following dialogue among the Senators is rapid, and their comments occasionally overlap.*)

SENATOR 1 (*looks through the telescope, looks up, turns the instrument around, wipes it gently with his sleeve, turns it back, and looks again*): It is not painted on the glass! The inscription on Sancta Maria; exactly as from the piazza! The same words and equally clear.
SENATOR 2: How? Venice is miles away. Let me look. (*takes the telescope*) The gondolas. (*He points his finger without taking his eye from the telescope, although no one else can possibly see what he intends to indicate.*) There, the same gondolas which carry my workers to the glassworks at Murano. With this I could observe from my own bedroom. The foreman cheats. I know it. Now I can count them myself. How much . . .
SENATOR 3 (*claiming his turn by nudging Senator 2 away . . . pauses*): It sees. It really sees. (*moves telescope slightly to the right, stares again*) Perhaps I should caution my wife to shutter her rooms.
SENATOR 4: The Professor has loftier concerns.
SENATOR 3 (*moves telescope again, smiling broadly*): Your wife, too, Fabricio.
SENATOR 4 (*reaches for telescope*): Let me see.

GALILEO (*whispering to Sagredo*): They are lovers ... but fortunately not today.
SAGREDO (*looks down*): The two wives? (*Galileo shrugs with a tolerant half-smile, then resumes writing.*)
SENATOR 1: A prodigy of invention.
SENATOR 4: Without question. (*lowering his voice*) But the amount ...
GALILEO (*to Sagredo, indignantly*): They debate my value!
SAGREDO: Merchants' habit, not presumption. To them goods are merely an emblem of value.
GALILEO: Even goods they do not understand.
SAGREDO: Those especially. It is their only refuge from the unfamiliar. (*He leaves the table and initiates an apparently intense conversation with Salviatti.*)
GALILEO (*muttering to Mazzoleni and Maria Celeste*): Look. Their excitement over a toy.
MARIA CELESTE: A construction of genius, my lord.
GALILEO: Ingenious, perhaps, but still a toy. Within a week, Mazzoleni will have improved my work. Let us show my daughter, Marcantonio. (*He reaches out.*)

(*Mazzoleni hands the lens which he has been polishing to Galileo, who fondles it tenderly before studying it closely.*)

GALILEO: Almost perfect. You see, Maria, how delicate a touch he has, far more skilled than my own. (*more jovially lest he sound condescending*) But we are not just toy makers—eh, Mazzoleni? Within this room we construct vessels that bear us far beyond the walls of Venice.
SALVIATTI (*to Senators*): A marvel? Truly. But more—much more—a weapon.
SENATOR 3: How, Filippo?
SAGREDO (*keeping his attention focused on the group at the window*

and speaking in a low tone that mutes but does not conceal his excitement): He has them! I think Filippo has them.

(*The Venetian Senators have been attentively waiting for Salviatti to elaborate on his claim. As Salviatti begins to talk an impatient Senator interrupts.*)

SENATOR 1: A weapon? Of course. It's obvious. With this we can see approaching ships long before they sight our harbor. (*pauses*) How long?
SALVIATTI (*looks around at Galileo, who does not look up, then turns back*): The Professor has calculated you would have two full hours' advantage. With help, he could construct instruments of even greater power.
SENATOR 3: He shall have whatever he needs.
SENATOR 2: Within reason, of course. If we spend everything to defend ourselves, we shall have nothing to defend. (*He laughs uncertainly, looks around, but none join him in laughter.*)
SENATOR 3: Shall the defense of the Republic be degraded by haggling over mere ducats?
SENATORS: No! . . . of course not . . . whatever the price.
SENATOR 3: Did I not tell you? I told you. Remember when the Senate debated, I told you—in the presence of the Doge himself—I prophesied, quite clearly, that a professor of mathematics would prove a wise investment.
GALILEO (*to Sagredo*): It is as you foretold. The somber guardians of our state will rank me among the nobles of philosophy, while excluding from evidence (*shaking manuscript*) the chiefmost yield of all my labors. (*Galileo falls silent as Sagredo returns to the Senators, his mounting inward ferocity betrayed only by a tightening grip on the manuscript. Suddenly his voice shifts into a low angry tone.*) This is the weapon.
SAGREDO: I do not doubt your work's importance to philosophy.

GALILEO (*falling silent*): My closest friends. And yet they do not know me.
SAGREDO (*turning back to Galileo, exultantly*): It is a triumph.
GALILEO: And the money?
SAGREDO: All you requested, and more.
GALILEO: Ten years of unremitting poverty, over! Gone! And for what? The labor of five days. A contrivance assembled in less than a week.

(*Sagredo and Salviatti join the cluster of Senators before Galileo has completed his last sentence. The exchanges among the Senatorial group, although animated, are only intermittently audible. They speak in low, indistinct tones.*)

—Naturally we must make some arrangement.
—Quite delicate: To be fair, yet not arouse envy.
—Such high distinction for a man who lives (*pauses, searching for euphemism*) not with a wife. I find it quite proper. For myself . . . no, not myself. I mean my moral self . . . I am married. That's it. I'm married but would not mind being unmarried . . . not me, but others . . . I myself would have no other wife. But those we govern have less generous views. (*lowers voice still more after looking around to make sure none of the household is listening*) And the child.
SAGREDO: Exactly. If the household is not proper, we *must* elevate him. How else shall such flagrant impropriety be sustained? His child is a holy sister. If heaven accepts, can Venice reject?
—Dispute the will of heaven? Not me . . . never.
—We could sell these instruments.
—Our profit would equal our payments.
—More . . . even more . . . much more.
SAGREDO: Remember, no ties of birth bind him to us. He is a man of Florence, his family descended from three centuries of nobility.

(*Salviatti, followed closely by Sagredo, walks toward the table.*)

SALVIATTI (*smiling triumphantly, putting his hand on Galileo's arm*): Done!
SAGREDO (*to Galileo*): I should bring them to you. (*Galileo nods. Salviatti returns to the group and accompanies them back to the table.*) Signor Galileo—
SENATOR 2 (*interrupting*): My congratulations, and, yes, my admiration, for your achievement. (*The other Venetians seem a bit uncomfortable.*) When we paid for a mathematician, we did not expect to fame Venice with so glorious a magician, who—like the sun itself—would uncurtain the unseen with comprehending light. (*The other Senators are embarrassed by this pomposity.*)
GALILEO (*obviously subduing anger*): I know nothing of magic. We (*indicating Mazzoleni*) shape the lens to bend the dispersed rays of light to a single point of focus; the proper curve is dictated by precise mathematical laws.
SENATOR 2 (*extending his hands and making a motion as if breaking a stick*): Bend the light? Aren't you afraid it might break?

(*A few of the other Senators laugh softly, despite their annoyance.*)

SAGREDO (*interrupting*): I am sure Signor Galileo will explain his work. We must proceed with ours; the day is fading. (*Others nod or mumble agreement and become silent.*) Signor Galileo. (*his tone now measured, official*) Tonight, the Senate of the Venetian Republic, with the concurrence of his Serene Highness, will designate you an honorary citizen of the Republic and professor for life with a salary of no less than one thousand scudi per annum. (*He pauses, looking at Galileo, who, without taking his eyes from Sagredo, appears somewhat somber, somewhat distracted, as if his thoughts had drifted to another topic.*) Subject, of course, to your acceptance. (*Galileo*

remains silent, his expression unchanged, until Salviatti, who has slipped behind the table, nudges him as if from a reverie.)
GALILEO: It is a great honor.
SENATOR 2 (*relieved*): For us.
OTHERS: Truly . . . for Venice . . . a good thing.
SAGREDO (*to others*): You must hasten to prepare the assembly.

(The Senators file out, nodding to Galileo, mumbling phrases of admiration, gratitude, and other well-mannered sentiments.)

SCENE SEVEN

(Galileo, who rose as his visitors left, is standing at the table clenching and unclenching his fist. He speaks in the unnaturally subdued and measured manner of one whose tensions betray the suppression of great passion.)

GALILEO: So. I am pledged (*smashing his fist on the table, the force of the blow scattering some of his papers, which Maria Celeste scrambles to retrieve*) to squander my scant hours on lessons for children! I need three more lives and have less than one, less than half of one. I, Galileo, already a destitute of time, must allow this tax on my poverty and pretend to gratitude . . .

(He sinks down into his chair, his force dissipated, head resting on an open hand. There is a brief silence, a frozen tableau.)

SAGREDO: Why did you leave?
GALILEO (*looking up, puzzled*): Leave? I accepted. You heard.
SAGREDO: Florence. You were an instructor there when you accepted the appointment of Venice.

GALILEO: My contract was for three years.
SAGREDO: And could not be renewed?
GALILEO: No. (*He pauses, reflectively, then begins speaking as if to himself, gradually turning and directing his words to Sagredo.*) I had some enemies, other teachers. They complained . . . how was it put? . . . that I was imbued with the spirit of contradiction. (*suddenly more spirited*) True, I put them to the test of debate, but never, never would I contradict others just to fortify my argument; only when they were wrong.
SAGREDO: Which was often.
GALILEO (*lifts his head and laughs*): Almost always, Sagredo. How did you know?
SAGREDO: That must have pleased them.
GALILEO: Those who took pleasure in quest for the truth.
SAGREDO: I have met few men in the universities of Italy who did not already know the truth.
GALILEO: You have met few philosophers. Why, an original man, the approach of an original man, even the rumor that such a man exists is received in the academies as if some old country priest had hobbled into the crowded bedchamber of a dying banker, carrying a frayed parish register to prove the indisputable bastardy of the expectant heir.
SAGREDO: Venice will nurture your fame. And free you to pursue your studies.
GALILEO: This outcast republic is a tomb for ideas. My message is for those who rule the Roman world. They are not found in Venice.
SALVIATTI: Nor in the Florence from which you came.
GALILEO: Not in Florence. From Florence.
SAGREDO: To Rome?
GALILEO: Whose voice hurdles all sovereign barriers.
MARIA CELESTE: Venice has never hindered your work. At times, it seemed you did nothing else. So many chill dawns, after matins,

I entered your room, to see only the cold, unbodied sheets which betrayed your night of solitary labor . . . passed here . . . at this table, where we had parted the day. You even had time to write a book. (*She points toward a rather slender manuscript on the table in front of Galileo.*)

GALILEO (*trying to change subject, leans over and strokes the girl's hair, his affectionate gesture immediately rewarded by a look of unmistakable adoration*): You have my father's eyes, and I hear his gifted love for music when you play the lute. You are right, Maria, my destination eludes me. Among all the envious tumults of the time, there are none to whisper in a sovereign's ear of what advantages an aging mathematician might bestow.

MARIA CELESTE (*proudly*): And a philosopher.

GALILEO (*puts finger on her mouth*): Only here. In this room. Elsewhere a man is honored with the title "philosopher" only when he soothes every curious itch with a balm extracted from a formula of Aristotle. In Milan, a new professor of philosophy is actually sworn on a volume of the master's work. A Bible too, of course. (*pauses in pretended thought*) I am not certain of the sequence.

MARIA CELESTE: You know Aristotle as well as anyone.

GALILEO: He is in my way.

SALVIATTI: Let me take your book. I will bring it home to Florence; a publisher will easily be found.

GALILEO: Thank you, Filippo, but I will keep it for now. It has taken me a decade of labor to describe just one tiny link in the mighty chain with which He binds the world.

(*The conversation is arrested. We hear the soft, crystalline singing of Maria Celeste as she strums her lute.*)

MARIA CELESTE: Praise Him, O children, in sound.
            Praise the good Jesus in song,

ACT ONE 51

Praise His thrice-holy name,
Which all the world adores.

(*Galileo, visibly relaxing, picks up a glass of wine, sips it, holds it in his mouth so it trickles slowly across his tongue, and swallows, looking pleased.*)

SALVIATTI: A wonderful wine.
GALILEO: A rich man's luxury but a poor man's necessity: the only pleasure he can share with kings.

SCENE EIGHT

(*Giovanni Ciampoli enters. Galileo rises swiftly to embrace him.*)

GALILEO: Giovanni.
CIAMPOLI: Master.
GALILEO (*drawing him toward the table*): You know my friends. Do you come from Rome?
CIAMPOLI: To Rome . . . from France, in the company of Cardinal Barberini. He is with the Archbishop and will join us shortly.
GALILEO: Barberini. The name is familiar. Is it possible I have met him?
CIAMPOLI: He was born in Florence a few years after you, the son of an old Tuscan family, like your own, though not so noble.
GALILEO: Nor as poor.
CIAMPOLI: The moment is great. The war for Europe has begun.
SAGREDO (*crossing himself, murmurs*): May God guide the imperial cross.
GALILEO: I knew this.
SAGREDO: You foresaw war? Something you read in the stars?

GALILEO: Nonsense.

SALVIATTI: But you do teach astronomy?

GALILEO: Not astronomy. I am required to teach poetry: a Greek lyric of whirling suns and crystal spheres and rings of celestial purity. No, through the progress of philosophy I sensed a trembling in the order of the world. I must go.

SAGREDO: Do you wish to enlist?

GALILEO: Not as a soldier. As armorer to the Holy Mother Church.

SAGREDO: And what weapons will you bring?

(*The door at the rear of the stage opens and Dr. Santerre Santorio, clearly excited, rushes in, then, seeing Galileo has guests, comes to an abrupt halt. The doctor is in his middle to late thirties, of medium height but of slighter frame than Galileo. Indeed, he might appear frail were it not for the ambient impression effused by the enthusiastic energy of his temperament. His beard is small and of triangular cut, more in the Spanish fashion, which he has also followed with a thin mustache which terminates in a slight upward curl. The result gives a slightly comic impression of a quite serious man. He is dressed in the formal garb of his profession. Under his right arm, the doctor carries a small wooden board to which he has nailed one end of a length of a string tied to a small piece of lead shaped like a fishing sinker. The suspended weight hangs alongside the doctor's leg. Obviously surprised by the presence of Galileo's visitors, he halts abruptly, stumbles, regains his balance, secures his burden, and bows with a kind of comic dignity.*)

GALILEO: I will bring this. (*indicating board*)

SAGREDO: A sight to make the Germans quake.

SANTORIO: I thought your visitors had left. (*starts turning as if to leave*)

GALILEO (*motioning him to enter*): These are my friends. (*As he reaches toward the board, Santorio edges away, seemingly embarrassed. Galileo reassures him.*) They share our passion for philosophy. (*San-*

torio's hesitation diminishes. *He completes his entrance, his formal manner gradually returning to the unguarded excitement of his entry. Galileo gestures toward him while looking toward those seated at the table.*) Dr. Santerre Santorio. (*The doctor nods.*) This is the noble Giovanni Sagredo, and beside him, Filippo Salviatti, equally noble. (*They acknowledge the introduction with a nod.*) You know Ciampoli.

(*Reaching for the board, Galileo holds his hand out to Santorio, who instinctively responds as if to shake hands, causing the board to slip and fall to the floor. Santorio lunges to catch it with his left hand, a gesture that brings him almost to his knees, then rises to an upright posture, the board now in his hand. Without the slightest sign of embarrassment at his clumsiness, he hands it to Galileo. Galileo holds aloft the coarse, unfinished board to which is nailed a length of ordinary household string fastened to a shapeless piece of lead. It seems crude and primitive alongside the instruments whose delicate symmetries grace Galileo's table.*)

GALILEO: This is a . . . (*He stops, looks at Santorio, waiting for him to provide the name. Santorio hesitates, reluctant, but Galileo does not take his eyes from the doctor's face.*)
SANTORIO (*slightly confused, calming himself, and speaking with calm, almost pedagogical dignity*): A pusilogium. (*falls silent, Galileo looking at him encouragingly*) It is to measure the patient's pulse. (*then with rising, almost excited enthusiasm*) Marvelous. Almost a miracle . . . don't you think so?
GALILEO (*looking at Santorio and speaking in a low tone*): They know nothing of medicine . . . perhaps, I should . . . it would be better. (*Santorio's expression shows acquiescence that Galileo assume the task of exposition.*)
GALILEO: Dr. Santorio's invention—
SANTORIO: Not mine, yours, Professor Galileo.

GALILEO: Yours.

SANTORIO (*to group at table*): We have no dispute. Please, understand it is not an argument. My confused expression is at fault. I did build it. But after the Professor's instruction.

SALVIATTI: You were the hands of the inventor.

SANTORIO: Exactly right.

GALILEO: Exactly wrong. The good-hearted doctor, thinking to disclaim credit, strips me of any triumph. This (*holding up the board*) is the firstborn of my new science.

SALVIATTI (*contemptuous*): That. A string fixed to a board. Anyone . . . I could do it myself.

GALILEO: Truly, Filippo. Have you ever hammered a nail? . . . No matter. It is easily learned. (*holds up hammer*) One end is to be held in the hand. The other strikes the nail. But with the flat side . . . the distinction is important. After that come a few refinements—the strength and length of the blow, how to support the nail while avoiding the fingers. But that comes quickly with practice. Does it not, Mazzoleni?

SAGREDO: You cannot persuade our minds to reject what our eyes can see. There is no resemblance between this crude pusil . . . pisilogy . . . this thing and those other instruments of most intricate design (*pointing to the instruments on Galileo's worktable*) for which Venice has paid so dearly.

GALILEO: Nor between them and the far more delicate architecture of a spider's web, which can be acquired by any housewife without the slightest expense.

SAGREDO: Meaning?

GALILEO: That either we give up our chairs of philosophy to spiders or you must abstain from judging philosophy by the artistry of its effects.

SALVIATTI (*a little impatiently*): Tell us then, this marvel of craftsmanship, how does it work?

ACT ONE

(Galileo holds the board so that the string and weight are suspended in a straight vertical line toward the floor. He then gives the weight a slight push which starts it swinging back and forth along the arc of a pendulum. He looks carefully at the swinging weight, then notices that his auditors are leaning forward, their eyes fixed in strained anticipation. In the moment of silence that ensues, the bell tower from a nearby monastery sounds the call to vespers, the repetition of its tones almost synchronized with each reversal of the weight's direction. Galileo remains silent, as his auditors wait, expectantly.)

GALILEO: That's all. Nothing more.
SALVIATTI (*looking up in surprise*): That's what it does? Nothing else?
GALILEO (*looking at the pendulum*): Did you expect it to take wing or, even better, change our wine to gold? It does have one quite remarkable property. Notice it swings along an arc, a segment of a circle. Each full journey along that arc will take exactly the same time. If we change the arc by, for example, shortening the string, it will swing faster, but always in obedience to the same command. It travels through equal arcs in equal times. The doctor, by comparing his patient's pulse to the motion of the pendulum, can tell if it is faster than normal . . . This rude device can measure time.
SALVIATTI: This discovery . . . when was it made?
GALILEO: During mass.
SALVIATTI (*puzzled*): Some implication from Scripture?
GALILEO: Several years ago, at the cathedral in Florence, I noticed one of the great chandeliers had been set in motion by a gust of wind. Finding the sermon tedious, I began to compare the swinging lamps with the beat of my pulse and found, amazingly, that each journey took the same number of beats, even as the distance diminished.

SAGREDO (*leans forward and reaches as if he were going to take the weight*): What is it made of?

GALILEO: It does not matter. Any weight—a stone, a block of wood, a scrap of metal—will behave the same. The principle of motion is not found inside the object. It is decreed by the law of pendulums. (*places the pusilogium on the table and picks up the hammer*) The lead has weight and shape, qualities our senses can perceive. But the swinging motion, where is it? Perhaps inside. (*He holds up the hammer as if to crush the weight. Salviatti lifts a restraining hand. Galileo, smiling, puts the hammer down.*) Quite right. Philosophy has endowed this object with qualities it does not possess. Why are we warmed at the winter hearth? Because it is the nature of fire to give heat. Why do birds fly? Because it is the nature of birds to fly. Our scholars explain the wonders of nature by naming them. That done, the mystery is solved, and the author is entombed among the illustrious of our land.

SAGREDO: You are unfair. Philosophers study objects to find the nature of objects.

GALILEO: And we learn . . . ?

SAGREDO: Well, as example, the nature of stone is to move earthward; of fire and smoke toward the heavens.

GALILEO: We learn nothing. Worse than nothing! (*picks up a small stone and drops it on the floor*) There! We, too, observe nature, which does not seem to have altered its behavior since Aristotle. You have just seen what he saw and can now confirm his immense discovery: a stone, once dropped, will fall.

SAGREDO: Do you jest at the ancients or at us?

GALILEO: Neither, I am teaching. Not the ancients. You. They, unhappily, are disabled from dialogue. (*looks upward*) Or so it is thought.

SAGREDO: As you know, better than I, the stone is merely an illustration.

GALILEO: Of what?
SAGREDO: The nature of stones and, by extension, of all heavy objects.
GALILEO (*throwing the stone forcibly to the ceiling*): Look, it rises? . . . Should I place it in a catapult, it would first rise, then fall, traveling an arc. If I dropped it from the mast of a moving ship it would strike the deck below, traveling down from the hand and forward with the ship. The conclusion? The only possible conclusion: this stone . . . perhaps all stones . . . has many natures: a dropping nature, a catapult nature, a shipboard nature. And there are other qualities, equally miraculous. Should I throw it at you —which I do not intend to do—we would discover a hurting nature; although if it were pumice, stroked gently across your back by a beautiful woman, you would discover still another nature, one more appropriate to the passionate pleasures of philosophic knowledge.
SAGREDO (*pointing out window*): You would have us believe nature is compounded of confusion?
GALILEO: The contrary. Of perfect order, whose beauty of proportion testifies to its origin with the Divine.

(*Cardinal Barberini strides into the room, his formal ecclesiastical garb making him the dominant figure in the room. He looks around quickly, then walks directly to Galileo and extends his hand, which Galileo kisses. Barberini immediately lifts him to his feet.*)

BARBERINI: So this is the great man, Giovanni. Your friend. Excuse my dress, but I come from an audience with the Archbishop.
GALILEO: Maria, a chair for His Reverence (*looks questioningly*) and a glass.
BARBERINI (*seated, looking intently at Maria*): Are you not young for

orders? I thought it not allowed . . . to choose such sacred union while still a child.
MARIA CELESTE: My father received a special dispensation.
BARBERINI (*turning to Galileo*): She is your daughter. Very beautiful.
GALILEO: The decision caused much pain. My labors allowed no leisure for the burdens of family.
BARBERINI: Nor do mine.
MARIA CELESTE: I serve God and my father, both.
BARBERINI: May that fortunate harmony give you everlasting joy. (*makes brief sign of benediction over her bowed head; looks up and sees telescope*) So, that is it. The talk of Venice. (*He rises, starts toward the window, looks back toward Galileo.*) May I?
GALILEO: Please, Your Reverence. (*goes to help him*)
BARBERINI (*looking through the glass*): Tremendous. I must send one to Richelieu. It can see Spaniards as well as Italians, can it not? (*turns, sees other instruments on table*) These strange marvels, are they also your creations?

(*Galileo accompanies Barberini to the worktable, which is cluttered with various tools and constructions of glass, wood, and metal. He picks up a glass object whose base is like that of a wine goblet supporting not an open cup but a hollowed glass sphere which opens, at its top, into a glass tube of very small diameter, about three-eighths of an inch, rising vertically for about one and a half inches before narrowing into a graceful spiral tube, about one-eighth of an inch in diameter, whose twelve turns enclose a diameter slightly smaller than the supporting sphere. The spiral terminates in a somewhat wider vertical glass tube, which itself turns into another glass sphere about a quarter the size of the first. The construction has been formed by working a single silicon mass into an unusual shape of geometric grace. The larger sphere is partly filled with a liquid whose slightly pinkish cast suggests water mixed with a few drops of wine.*)

GALILEO: This is my thermoscope. It measures differences of heat and cold. Cupped thus, the fluid, emboldened by my warmth, will rise, in defiance of its natural level.
BARBERINI: Ingenious. And this? (*pointing*)

(*Galileo picks up a somewhat cruder construction consisting of a partly open small glass bowl from the center of which rises a thin vertical glass tube.*)

GALILEO: This measures the weight of air. (*He sets it down.*) It needs refinement. (*Turning, he sees the slightly puzzled expressions of his other guests and smiles.*) You didn't know air had weight, as water does? (*They return to the group.*)
BARBERINI: Ciampoli, you misled me. You did not tell me your friend was an artist as well as a philosopher.
CIAMPOLI: And each talent serves the other.
BARBERINI: Extraordinary. There is none else. (*pauses*) None living. There was Leonardo. Also born in Florence.
CIAMPOLI: It is his genius and the barrier to his genius. Men who use their hands to feed their minds are suspect to our narrow age.
BARBERINI: We anticipate more spacious times.
SAGREDO: Ciampoli has informed us.
BARBERINI: Ah! The turmoil of the times. New rulers, new ambitions, new terrors.
SAGREDO: A world of armies would not seem a place of refuge either for philosophers or for artists.
BARBERINI: They would be wise to keep a distance. But later. Once the power of heresy is broken. Lasting restoration will require a Rome purified, and host to the creations of beauty and wisdom. But I preach to the converted, an unfortunate habit, acquired in France. What were you discussing?
SALVIATTI: Aristotle. We were discussing Aristotle.
GALILEO: Maria, bring me some ice. (*Maria leaves, returning with a*

piece of ice while Galileo continues.) Aristotle teaches that ice is compressed water. If he is right, ice is heavier than water. (*He takes the ice from Maria and throws it into a pitcher of water. All look in fascination as the ice comes to the surface and floats.*) So much for Aristotle, and so much for the mimicking disciples of two thousand years. Unless you think some Greek spirit has entered this room to delude our senses or support the ice.

BARBERINI (*applauding, aside to Ciampoli*): The man has force. (*to the group*) It is settled, then. There is no contest from Scripture, is there, Giovanni?

CIAMPOLI: The inhabitants of Judea had little experience with ice.

BARBERINI: You must visit Rome. Later I will introduce you at the Collegio Romano, where you can find a warm audience for your novelties of philosophy. For now, philosophize in your study, Galileo, and await your time. It shall come.

GALILEO: I fear it passes.

BARBERINI: I understand. It is difficult for wisdom to gain an audience in a city of merchants. (*leans close to Galileo, whispering*) Teachings from Venice are unlikely to find favor in Rome. The Venetian Senate has defied orders from the Holy Office and expelled the Jesuits. (*louder*) Perhaps Florence?

GALILEO: They have refused me.

BARBERINI: Have they? I have some influence with the Grand Duke. After all, we are both men of Florence.

SAGREDO: I hope you see the wisdom of the Cardinal's counsel. History has fallen to the direction of practical men. They have no leisure for philosophy.

GALILEO: Wrong, Sagredo! Utterly, fatefully, wrong! It is I who am the practical man. Look. (*He picks up two small pieces of wood from the table, throws them up, and lets them fall back to the table.*) They rush upward in opposition to the attraction of the earth, and then they fall. A trifle. Every street juggler can do as much. Yet the movement of those wooden blocks—like the motion of all

substance—is governed by laws as precise, as terrible in their inevitability, as those which compel the celestial bodies.
SALVIATTI: These laws, have you recorded them?
GALILEO: In this book (*indicates manuscript*), but only the few I have learned. Yet enough so that given the weight of any object and the force which propels it, I can calculate its descent—the place and time of its arrival.
SALVIATTI: Even for cannon or catapult?
GALILEO: The mathematics are the same.
BARBERINI (*to Ciampoli*): Ideas that can be forged into weapons. A novelty. Perhaps more useful than I imagined. (*to Galileo*) I would gladly remain here as your student. But Giovanni can tell me of your achievements. For now I must obey a summons, most imperative, and most unlikely to be repeated. (*He rises to leave.*)
CIAMPOLI: Master, accept the Cardinal's advice. We will meet again, and that occasion, perhaps, may yield more than sympathetic admiration. (*They depart.*)

SCENE NINE

(*Galileo is seated at his table, obviously disturbed. There are a few moments of silence as his friends watch him questioningly.*)

GALILEO: There was no time to make him understand.
SAGREDO: You spoke of the celestial bodies. Do they also have laws?
GALILEO: The heavens are not a completely safe subject for investigation in our age. But tell me, Sagredo, why the laws of motion should be any different in the furthest reaches of the celestial sphere than on this table.
SAGREDO: Because the heavens are unlike our globe, being eternal, fixed, and unchanging witness to the corruptions of earth.

GALILEO: How do you know?

SAGREDO: By experience. We see waters drown the land, earth sundered by consuming flame, dismal decline and painful birth. No such corruptions are witnessed in the heavens.

GALILEO: You have not seen corruptions in China or America. Are China and America celestial spheres?

SAGREDO: The heavens manifest the wonders of God. Not the mind of Galileo.

GALILEO: Do you think to glorify the Divine by belief that God's angels, or perhaps God Himself, must continually push the stars and planets along their path. Might it be more pious to believe the Almighty has created a simple law of mathematics which frees Him and his servants from any further concern for the ordered movement of the universe and all it contains?

SAGREDO: Many others have observed nature and found no laws.

GALILEO: I do not observe nature. I question nature.

SAGREDO: And it answers you . . . here . . . this stone . . . (*points to telescope*) the glass . . . (*points out window*) the trees, perhaps, and the soft hills of Tuscany.

GALILEO: You think me lunatic! I ask by measuring, as with the pendulum . . . or by comparing an object's weight with its speed of fall.

SAGREDO: Ingenious, the questions. But to hear answers, a miracle.

GALILEO (*holds up Bible*): The Bible . . . the words of God . . . you understand them. It is written in a language you know. God's works are also inscribed in this grand book we call the universe, continually before us, to be understood by all who learn the language and the characters in which it is written: the language of mathematics, whose characters are triangles, circles, and other shapes of geometry.

SAGREDO: You would be wise to omit comparisons between your calculations and those of God.

GALILEO: Nonsense. If I have discovered the language of nature it

is because of our Catholic faith, which teaches its children of God's infinite love. It is He who gave us senses and the power of reason. It is not in the nature of Divine love to bestow such powers only then to deceive and mock our efforts to understand His creation.
MARIA CELESTE: Perhaps the Almighty has chosen to place His Creation beyond our understanding, so eternal mystery will testify to His rule.
GALILEO (*voice softening*): That is a possibility, my dear.
MARIA CELESTE (*speaking to herself, but in a ringing tone that draws attention*): "The secret things," Moses said, "belong to the Lord our God."
SALVIATTI: If you have learned to question nature and to read its answers . . . why? . . . why you?
GALILEO: I do not know.
SAGREDO: Do you think yourself chosen—
GALILEO: Not for any special virtue of my own. It is the time. He has chosen His time. (*smiles benignly, but clearly absorbed in his own thoughts: then with mounting excitement*) You must try to understand. This new philosophy is not a citizen of Venice or of Italy. It is not baptized Catholic. A man in England finds wondrous forces in the behavior of a magnet; Kepler in Prague replaces the perfect celestial circle with orbits shaped like an egg.
SAGREDO: Do they know more than you?
GALILEO: Less. Much less. But others will come. First a handful, and then an army, a host of discoverers who will direct the course of human culture for centuries to come. (*pauses*) I am a man with a message but without a voice.
SAGREDO: Would you transform the world?
GALILEO: Not the world. The mind of man by which the world is known.
SAGREDO: I cannot fully understand the philosophy of Galileo. I do not even try. Shall the mouse make the measure of the elephant? Yet, if all this is true, even to the utmost, these discoveries will

not conduct you to Florence. You have made your philosophy from words and numbers, for a race which learns, if at all, with reluctant labor. Fame comes swiftly only for discoveries that our senses can apprehend—the naked Indians who amazed the sight of approaching Columbus; gold freshly dredged from Peruvian mines. These are discoveries which fever the imagination, excite poets to tribute, kings to honor. Disprove an idea unchallenged for two thousand years, the world yawns. But carry wine of unexpected pleasures from some Pacific island, and you become a hero to Europe. Philosophy alone cannot gratify the insistent appetite of the ignorant for wonders and marvels.

GALILEO: Why not? Why can it not? (*Galileo looks toward Salviatti, who is made inarticulate by the unexpected reaction.*) Wonders and marvels. You are right, absolutely right. Then wonders and marvels it must be. Filippo, you have taught me something today. I am grateful.

SALVIATTI (*to Sagredo, who stares, unmoving, as if mesmerized by Galileo*): You must prepare the assembly.

SAGREDO (*shaking his head as if to rid it of a passing fly*): Of course. (*He rises from the table, as does Salviatti. They move toward the door.*) Galileo, you do not make things easy for your friends.

GALILEO: Or for myself.

SAGREDO: Why did you choose so painful a profession? Such immense force, in an artist, would attract bids from every court in Europe.

GALILEO: I lacked the gift.

SAGREDO: I have heard that your father, Vincenzio, insisted your musical genius could have surpassed his own.

GALILEO: My father's vanity extended to all his creations. But his paternal love urged me toward the study of medicine.

SAGREDO: Why?

GALILEO: My dear Sagredo, how innocently you betray your ignorance of poverty. When I chose mathematics, a study neither practical nor entertaining, my father foresaw the completion of our shame: one of the noblest families of Tuscany declined to a tribe of beggars. (*With a casual sweep of his arm, Galileo gestures to indicate his entire surroundings.*) You see, I am descended from a prophet as well as an artist.

SAGREDO: Did he oppose you?

GALILEO: Only at first. Then . . . it is fresh as yesterday in my mind. The day he first admitted Ostilio Ricci—a young instructor whom I had persuaded to tutor me in mathematics. We were seated in the music room, silent, when the sound of poor Master Ricci's rather timid knock propelled my father toward me. His hands closed on my shoulders (*Galileo rubs his shoulders as if he can still feel the grip*), imprisoning me within the intensity of those probing eyes. Then . . . it was only a moment . . . I felt his grip soften, saw the beams disperse: "It is me," he said. "There behind the bone. I am looking into a mirror. No. Not a mirror. Not just a mirror. Some magician's crystal which magnifies most mightily the image it reflects. I have hurled my entire career against the authority which would confine music to numbers and ratios, to constructs of theory taken from logic instead of sound. But it is not my defiance I see . . . yet is also that . . . I see it, and I do not see.

"I have hurled a stone or two against the ramparts of our ignorance. But you . . . you, my son. Your soul prepares an avalanche that would not shrink to make all Europe one Pompeii. Go. You are impatient. Go to your Master Ricci. Poor man. He believes himself your teacher. And so he is. As the wine cup is master of the feast."

Then, as I left, he shouted after me, "Become a mathematician. Play with your numbers, so you can spend your life scraping fees from the condescending fathers of contentious boys. Is that what you want? You want to be poor? Then go, go and live in poverty." And suddenly, I can still hear it, the sudden stricken softening of

his voice: "May God guard you . . . my passionate son . . . my boy . . . my Galileo. You have the blessings of your father."
SAGREDO: Your father was a wise man.
GALILEO: But inclined to extravagance of expression.
SAGREDO: Perhaps.

(*Sagredo and Salviatti exit, accompanied by Santorio.*)

SCENE TEN

(*Beyond Galileo's windows a few faint streaks of red reflected from neighboring buildings are the final withdrawing ensigns of the retreating sun. During the next few minutes, they will fade as day yields its watch to night. Galileo and Mazzoleni are seated at the table which Maria and her mother have been preparing for dinner during the preceding scene.*)

GALILEO: Wonders and marvels. Not so simple, is it, Mazzoleni?
MAZZOLENI: You made it seem so.
GALILEO: Pretense. Harmless bravado. You know that.

(*As Galileo speaks, the area illuminated by the stage lights begins to shrink, gradually enveloping the rest of his household in shadow, until, by the end of his speech, one sees only Galileo, illuminated by a single cone of light and, through the windows, the profound darkness of the evening sky.*)

GALILEO: Mathematics is not a magician. It cannot cause nuns to float on air, foretell a successful seduction, or, like Joshua, prolong the day by halting the sun's descent. (*laughs softly, almost to himself*) It was not the sun that stood still that day, was it, Mazzoleni? Old Copernicus taught us that. There is a marvel, a true marvel—at his desk, on the edge of shivering Poland. Copernicus. Uncovering the true design of God's own universe. Still the greatest of all questions. Perhaps my philosophy could confirm Copernicus. If it could accomplish that. But how. So far away, the heavens, like some China of the skies. (*pauses, musing*) I remember, as a boy, lying in bed, hearing my father's friends argue about music—what proportions and ratios, which mathematical relations—were required of a composition. Then my father's voice, its roar drowning all debate: "Is it beautiful? Is that your dispute? *Then listen to the music!*"

(*There is a pause. Galileo looks through the window at the night sky beyond. Then, with sudden excitement, he leaps to his feet and rushes to the idle spyglass. The room is gradually enveloped in shadow, leaving only Galileo illuminated as he sits by the telescope. His chair, like those often seen in elementary schools, has an arm extending from its frame that widens to present a writing surface for the right hand of the occupant. The low seat allows Galileo a comfortable position from which to make his observations. As the lights diminish toward total darkness, we become aware—part sight, part intuition—that Galileo, his chair, and his telescope are revolving. There is an instant of total blackness before a cone of light reveals Galileo seated facing the audience, looking through a telescope, now pointed toward the theater ceiling, where there is projected an image of the night sky, as if the entire theater had been turned into a planetarium. To the limit of technical possibility, the image will change, giving prominence to the successive objects of his observation.*)

GALILEO: First? (*He pauses. A full moon is prominent in the night sky.*) The moon. Full-bottomed Eve: grafted by God as comfort to the fugitive earth. So ripe tonight. So swollen with sweet invitation. Do you mock the men you madden with unconsummate desire? I wonder. Let me see if I can peek beneath the hem of your borrowed radiance. (*a brief pause as Galileo continues to look through the telescope, and then sits back in his chair*) The dark spots. They are no mystery at all: only the cratered shadows of erupted rock. I have seen the valley of the Arno so enshrouded while the Tuscan hills still flamed with sun. (*begins to laugh*) That marbled sphere, that perfect crystal form of our philosophy, proves more erupt and fissured than our ravaged earth, itself no longer to be thought a corrupt and bastard outcast amid spheres of celestial purity, but in the company of celestial bodies, rivaling all the rest in splendor and in majesty, equal subject to the same decrees which govern all the natural universe. (*He laughs again.*)

So, Aristotle, after two thousand years, in a single night—in one hour of one single night—I have torn the keystone from the arch. (*in a commanding tone directed at the darkness behind him*) Paper! Pen! Quickly! I must publish my discoveries immediately. These observations must soon occur to someone else. (*returns to telescope*)

Next? (*pause*) The Milky Way. That baffling Mediterranean of light! It seems a rupturing gulf in the dark roof of the world. (*looks intently*) It is . . . they are . . . STARS! HUNDREDS! NO, THOUSANDS! TENS OF THOUSANDS! So closely packed that the eye could not distinguish! With one new world Columbus amazed all the thrones of Europe. I will bring them a million.

(*He picks up the pen, which along with some blank paper has appeared on the writing arm of his chair.*) How shall I title my discoveries? What word did Filippo use . . . about the geometry of my pendulum? "A message." And so is this . . . (*He leans over and starts to write.*) A Message from the Stars. (*He pauses, looks up, musing.*) Moon, Milky Way, and, yes, a planet. I need a planet to close the angle of this survey.

(*He reaches for the telescope, and looking through the eyepiece, moves it to scan the heavens.*) Jupiter. The House of Jupiter ascends.

(*We see projected the face of Jupiter, a compound of red vortices made familiar to us by our rockets of exploration. There are, in total, four "moons."*)

One . . . two . . . no, four. (*exuberantly*) Four planets, never before seen, captive to Jupiter as moon to Earth! (*removes his eye from the telescope*) By right of discovery, I can name them. (*pauses*) To honor the ruling house of Florence. From this night, for all eternity, they are to be known as the Stars of Medici. (*pauses, begins to smile*) If I have fashioned them a place in the heavens, surely they can find one at their court for me. (*He bends over the paper and resumes writing.*) Accept then, most clement prince, this gentle glory reserved by the stars for you.

(*Galileo is still, as he continues writing. In the silence we hear Maria Celeste as she strums the lute.*)

MARIA CELESTE: All things fall and are built again,
And those that build them are gay.
The ties that wind the world must part,
And be rewoven with a singing heart.

(*There is silence. Galileo puts down his pen and looks directly toward the audience.*)

GALILEO: I have seen more and further this night than all the sons of Adam.

(*He crosses himself. The stage darkens.*)

ACT TWO

(*Pictured on the right side of the closed curtain are the three participants in Galileo's still unwritten* Dialogue on the Two Chief World Systems. *On the left, behind the curtain, is the shadow of Maria Celeste, seated at a small writing table, holding a rose in her hand. She carefully puts down the flower and begins to write, speaking the words as she spells them out.*)

MARIA CELESTE: Dearest father, I send you this flower as token of my love. And with the rose you must accept its thorns, which represent the bitter passion of Our Lord.

(*Scenes 1–5 each take place in a different sector of the darkened stage, beginning at the far right and going counterclockwise. Scene 6 takes place at center stage. Each quadrant is illuminated, and then thrust back into darkness as the light moves to the next display.*)

SCENE ONE

(*On the far right we see a small stone residence whose balcony overlooks a cobblestone way in the city of Prague, nominal capital of the Holy Roman Empire. In the still sleeping streets, the last few fragments of retreating night linger in shadowed lintels, when a short, stout, but vigorous man—formally dressed in wide sacklike trousers, high spurred boots, flat white turned-down collars, and a large, plumed felt hat with an upturned brim—rides to the house and, in obvious agitation, pulls up his horse, dismounts—almost tumbles to the street—and shouts toward the shuttered doors of the balcony.*)

WACKHER: Kepler! Johannes Kepler! (*Receiving no response, he strains to reach a louder tone.*) Kepler! Are you there? It is me.

(*The balcony doors open and Johannes Kepler steps onto the balcony. He is an imposing presence. Unusually tall, his almost fleshless frame, full dark beard, and cavernous eyes make him appear more like an Oriental prophet than a German scientist—an impression reinforced by his dressing gown, whose silken whiteness curves along a gentle arc from his shoulders to the balustrade, dazzling in contrast to the grays and browns of the German neighborhood. An ignorant stranger—had *one chanced to pass—might well have thought him a wizard or the apparition of a wizard. With his left hand, Kepler shields his eyes from the rising sun; his right hand holding a somewhat more bulky and less ornamented version of Galileo's spyglass.*)

KEPLER: So it is the most illustrious Lord Wackher of Wackenfels. I was about to summon guards.

WACKHER: Is it true, Kepler? Is it true?

KEPLER: Is what true?

WACKHER: What all Prague talks about. Some Italian has discovered four new planets.

KEPLER (*with a gravity of tone and manner, unnaturally heightened by his effort to suppress laughter*): I have read his book. But I cannot say that I have observed them.

WACKHER: They say he has invented an instrument to extend the eyes.

KEPLER: Nonsense! (*At this, Wackher looks downcast.*) It does not magnify our senses, but the objects presented to them.

WACKHER (*brightening, but uncertain*): Then there is such an invention.

KEPLER: The principle is discussed in my book of optics. (*looking at Wackher sternly*) Which you told me you had read.

WACKHER: Most of it. Most of it. Some parts were too technical. Then he has invented nothing?

KEPLER: The idea, no. But he actually built one, and directed it to the heavens. (*Wackher begins to speak and is interrupted by Kepler.*) Imagine, Wackher, for a thousand years we thought the mind alone could wrestle Nature's secrets from her concealing bosom. And all was mystery. Now God has found Himself a philosopher with hands, and we begin to uncertain the wonders of Creation. (*holds a telescope tube aloft*) And when I have finished this, we shall all see what Galileo saw. (*Wackher has begun to jump up and down, resembling a distended, sober-hued ball. Now he breaks into a cari-*

cature of a dance beneath Kepler's window. Kepler erupts with laughter, and lifts both hands toward the sky.) Can you hear it, Wackher? I can hear it. The laughter of old Copernicus, echoing across the vaults of heaven as he looks down, this redeeming day, on those who reviled and mocked him.
WACKHER: Incredible! Marvelous! That I should live to see it! (*remounts his horse*) I must tell the imperial court.
KEPLER (*still holding the telescope aloft, as Wackher rides off*): O telescope! More precious than a scepter! Is not he who holds thee in his hands made king and lord of the works of God?

SCENE TWO

(*The next tableau reveals the adolescent King Louis XIII seated in a thronelike chair, talking to Richelieu.*)

RICHELIEU (*patiently*): An injustice, Your Majesty. A flagrant injustice.
LOUIS: Rulers of Tuscany. A trivial Italian province. It isn't fair. Now we must see them glisten in the night sky far above us.
RICHELIEU: I believe them invisible to the eye, Your Majesty.
LOUIS: We *know* they are there. This astrologer . . . astronomer . . . Giorgio . . .
RICHELIEU: Galileo.
LOUIS: Quite right. Demand he name the next star after the House of Bourbon.
RICHELIEU: He is not our subject.
LOUIS: It is not to be borne.
RICHELIEU: But he might be persuaded.
LOUIS: You think so?

RICHELIEU: If the reward is generous enough; one that befits a king.
LOUIS: Compose a letter today. We must act quickly before some other Italian enters the heavens.
RICHELIEU (*turning to go, speaking partly to himself*): The heavens will be patient.
LOUIS (*calling after the departing Richelieu*): Perhaps not a planet. Not *just* a planet . . . a new sun. (*then musingly, to himself*) The sun of Bourbon. The Bourbon sun. (*calls out again to Richelieu*) My family is too large. Perhaps it should be named just for me . . . for the King of France . . . Louis the King.

SCENE THREE

(*The reemerging light discloses the youthful Cosimo II, Grand Duke of Tuscany, sitting carelessly, almost sprawled, in a gold-trimmed throne chair. He is twenty-four. Above the chair hangs Botticelli's "Birth of Venus." Cosimo is idly engrossed in conversation with Francesco Niccolini, his contemporary and friend, who is standing, partly turned from the audience and facing the Grand Duke. He holds a lute in his right hand. Cosimo is laughing—in all probability at some joke of Niccolini's.*)

COSIMO: Well deserved, Niccolini, now the song . . . may I hear it?
NICCOLINI (*sings while accompanying himself on the lute*):
        Your crest of Medici, unfurled,
        Rules this garden of the world.
        Beneath your wise and placid yoke,
        Beneath the flags you raise on high.

Gaily and without a sigh,
Proud Arno bows its willing head.

Cosimo: You think it extravagant?
Niccolini: No longer. What is the praise of tiny Tuscany to rulers now enthroned in heaven's night?
Cosimo: A great deal, when they must pass their days in Florence.
Niccolini: Will you offer Galileo a place at court?
Cosimo: Should I?
Niccolini: Without delay! Can you accept this gift yet refuse the giver?
Cosimo: Were they his to give?
Niccolini: By right of discovery.
Cosimo: The right, of course, but the power? Without power, right is just the whisper of desire.
Niccolini: Who can dispute him?
Cosimo: Nobody. Probably nobody.

(*Andrea Cigoli, Secretary of State, moves into the light from the margin of the tableau, opposite Niccolini. He is a man of advanced middle age and average stature whose humorless dignity verges on the pompous. Cosimo rises to greet him.*)

Cosimo: Minister Cigoli, you have examined the dispatches?
Cigoli (*hesitating, as the two other men wait expectantly, then drawing himself up as if he were about to make a proclamation before a large crowd*): The College of Rome has announced a banquet in his honor.
Cosimo (*clearly delighted with the news*): Anything else?
Cigoli: Galileo will receive a private audience with the Holy Father.
Cosimo: He deserves no less. (*He reaches back and takes a large white envelope from the chair on which he has been sitting and hands it to Cigoli.*) Send this to Galileo. (*turning toward Niccolini, exu-*

berantly) Well, my friend, we shall have the great one after all. (*Cigoli bows and turns to leave. As he moves away, Cosimo recalls him, then points to the painting over his chair.*) My grandfather was a great admirer of Botticelli. So am I. Still, given the times, something a touch more pious might be appropriate.

CIGOLI: I shall see to it, Your Majesty.

(*He exits, leaving the two younger men gazing at the naked Venus as the light goes down.*)

SCENE FOUR

(*A small, dimly lit chamber. We can scarcely see the profiled figure of a man, heavy and of medium stature, who sits behind a desk. He appears to be wearing ecclesiastical robes and, on his head, the small red domed cap of a cardinal of the Roman Curia. He is writing. Across from him, standing silently, fully lit, is a young priest, Father Tommaso Caccini, recently ordained into the Dominican order. His gray, concave, peaked features manifest little of the freshness or innocence of youth.*)

CARDINAL: Not just a philosopher. Chief philosopher to the Grand Duke of Tuscany. If his own philosopher is suspect to the church, Cosimo will be more zealous to demonstrate his obedience in other matters.

CACCINI: The loyal Duke would never defy Rome.

CARDINAL: The armies of Spain will march along the borders of northern Tuscany. Rome wishes no interference from a fearful Florence. (*pausing*) But such matters are not your concern. Your Superior recommended you as one energetic in obedience and ambition. Curiosity and wit were not mentioned.

CACCINI: I know no one in Florence. Shall I call on Archbishop Mazzimedici?
CARDINAL: No churchmen. Not yet. There is a certain Professor delle Colombe, a teacher of philosophy, much offended at Galileo's rise.
CACCINI: Is this Galileo so disliked?
CARDINAL: Of all hatreds, there is none greater than that of ignorance against knowledge. (*He hands him the paper on which he has been writing.*) Here is your safe-conduct. Destroy it when you cross the border.
CACCINI: When shall we meet again?
CARDINAL: Never! Have no concern. Your services will be remembered. (*Caccini turns and leaves.*) A perfection of his type. God's own villain.

SCENE FIVE

(*Cardinal Barberini sits at a simple uncarved table in the relatively austere surroundings of his temporary accommodations provided by the Vatican. He is writing slowly, with intense concentration. Ciampoli enters and pauses for a moment until Barberini becomes aware of his presence and looks up.*)

BARBERINI: Imagine, Giovanni, another day in Venice and we might have witnessed the discoveries. I could have brought him to Florence directly.
CIAMPOLI: We saw genius enough to justify intervention.
BARBERINI: Enough? If kings had minds! But they do have eyes. And your professor has lanterned the skies of Europe. It is a sign from God.

CIAMPOLI: The planets? They were always there.

BARBERINI: Not the stars. That the discoverer was an Italian, and the timing most fortunate. He must come to Rome.

CIAMPOLI: It would be best to wait until he is at the court of Florence and can come sponsored by his new sovereign.

BARBERINI: The imperial armies have desolated half of Protestant Europe and are already at the gates of Nuremberg. Should it fall, only a handful of troops will remain to contest their conquest of the continent.

CIAMPOLI: May the Lord be praised.

BARBERINI: Of course. And also beseeched that victorious armies will not turn toward Rome.

CIAMPOLI: A Rome torn between jubilation and fear will have little leisure for philosophy.

BARBERINI: Before we left Venice I spoke to the Admiral. Galileo increased the speed of the Venetian galleys simply by changing the seats of the oarsmen, and he did it with mathematics, using the sea and not the oarlock as the fulcrum of the stroke. We must have him. The man is a genius of invention.

CIAMPOLI: To him, inventions are the mere offspring of his philosophy, which he will propound in every Roman home.

BARBERINI: I have no objection to philosophy. But you must explain that Rome will not be ready to discuss the design of Creation until its own borders are secure. Counsel him to be patient.

CIAMPOLI: He is a passionate man.

BARBERINI: So am I. Go to him, Giovanni.

CIAMPOLI: I would not draw my friend into a trap.

BARBERINI: There is none. There is to be a banquet in his honor. And you can bring him this crude poem of my own composition (*picks up the paper he has been writing on and begins to read*):

> O brilliant ray, our Galileo's eye,
> Stirs up the sluggard in our ancient sky,

Where blind philosophers must grope and
     sigh . . .
Our Galileo's made the planets fly!
CIAMPOLI: There is a title?
BARBERINI: "Perniciosa Adulatio." Dangerous Admiration.
CIAMPOLI: Discoveries of philosophy, are they dangerous?
BARBERINI: There is always some danger in the new. More danger for the philosopher than for his admirers.

SCENE SIX

(*A momentary darkness, then a single spotlight shines on Johannes Kepler as he walks to center front, still wearing his long white dressing gown. In his left hand he carries a candle, in his right an open book, which he is reading silently as he walks. He comes to a stop and looks up toward the audience.*)

KEPLER: Now the ax is laid to the root of the tree.

(*He shuts the book decisively, leans over and blows out the candle, as bells begin their summons to matins. The stage is dark.*)

SCENE SEVEN

(*It is about five or six years later. We are at the spacious but meanly furnished house of Ludovici delle Colombe, located a few blocks from the Arno River, which cleaves and occasionally submerges the center of Florence. Delle Colombe, professor at the University of Pisa, is the acknowledged leader of the anti-Galileo group among the academicians* of Tuscany. He will achieve historical immortality because of the wholly fortuitous circumstance that his family name meant "pigeon," which, as debate mounted, proved an irresistible epigram for the diverse repositories of hostility toward the new philosophy. Many were to become "pigeons" who neither esteemed nor even knew delle Colombe. He stands, his left side toward the audience, addressing two men seated on a facing couch. Behind him are shelves or the suggestion of shelves holding his books. To his right, at stage rear, is Raphael's "Portrait of Leo X with Cardinal Giulio de Medici and Luigi de Rossi." It may well occur to acute observers that the three living men seem almost a cartoon of the dark and weighty trio who brood over the room.

(*Directly across from delle Colombe sits Father Magini, a professor of mathematics in Bologna, a position fairly won in competition with several well-qualified aspirants, including the younger Galileo. On the far corner of the couch, to delle Colombe's right, pressed against the cushions as if he were trying to obliterate his presence or at least conceal it, is Father Caccini.*)

DELLE COLOMBE: We taught together at Pisa.
CACCINI (*suddenly leaning forward, as if emerging from the shadows*): Why, then, Professor delle Colombe, did he go to Venice?
DELLE COLOMBE: Florence would not have him. He lacked reverence.
CACCINI: Perhaps just a young man anxious for attention.
DELLE COLOMBE (*holding up his copy of* Message from the Stars): He has certainly found it. He reinvents the universe.
MAGINI: You share my skepticism?
DELLE COLOMBE: It is a scandal to the profession of philosophy.
CACCINI: Have you made your own observations of the heavens?
MAGINI (*interjecting*): He has no spyglass.
DELLE COLOMBE: I need no broomstick. I am a professor, not a sorcerer. True philosophy journeys from here (*puts his hand on the*

books behind him) to here. (*He taps his skull, then suddenly begins to pace, sniffing loudly, like an animal tracking its prey.*) Do you smell it? (*sniffs*) The sea! But we are on land. I have it! The waters are blended with the firmament. Bring paper. I must write a book so the world can marvel that the Book of Genesis and Aristotle both were toppled by my nose.

CACCINI (*in a questioning tone*): Many philosophers have studied the heavens?

MAGINI (*turning toward him, heatedly*): There is no need for four new planets. The Divine design is complete without them.

DELLE COLOMBE (*breaking in excitedly*): Exactly. Since nature does nothing in vain, four new planets could have no possible purpose. Ergo (*triumphantly*), they do not exist. Nor are planets the limit of his mischief. Like some drunken cook, thinking to enrich his stew by pissing into the pot, Galileo has scrambled the purity of heavenly spheres with the corruptions of earth.

MAGINI (*disgustedly*): Mountains on the moon! Next, he will populate Jupiter with Turks.

DELLE COLOMBE: Find naked Amazons dancing on the sun.

CACCINI (*softly, almost to himself*): And where has he left a place for Christ?

DELLE COLOMBE: I will not concede his four new planets to that Italian from Padua, though I die for it.

CACCINI: Suppose you looked through his telescope.

DELLE COLOMBE (*in a tone of revulsion, rubbing his hands as if ridding them of filth*): Never.

CACCINI: And suppose further that you saw the four new planets. Would you be satisfied?

DELLE COLOMBE: Yes. I would be satisfied. That he painted them on the glass.

CACCINI: What will you do?

DELLE COLOMBE: I shall exterminate him. (*Both men look startled.*) With my new book. (*holds up manuscript*)

CACCINI: You choose his weapon. There are other ways. We may enlist more powerful adversaries.
DELLE COLOMBE: From Rome.
CACCINI: From Scripture. I have invited a friend who may help us.

(*Father Niccolo Lorini, another Dominican and a professor of ecclesiastical history at Florence, is announced. Although Lorini is quite elderly, his many years have not multiplied his understanding of natural philosophy or science. Unfortunately, his holy zeal for the Church and established authority is inversely proportional to his knowledge and intellect. Although comic, even ridiculous, to the observer, he will be a fatal antagonist. Lorini is greeted with a show of deference which obviously pleases him.*)

DELLE COLOMBE: You share our fears of the novelties which intrigue the fashionable of Florence?
LORINI: Only a month ago, I preached a sermon opposed to new ideas of philosophy. The Archbishop . . . strangely, he seemed upset. I explained I had been asked about the new doctrines, so I had to say something lest I appear a fool—not about astronomy, of course. It is not my field . . . only Scripture . . . that the doctrines of that Polish fellow, Ipericus, were contrary to Holy Scripture.
CACCINI: *Copernicus* is answered by Solomon: "The sun comes forth . . . and like a giant, joyfully runs its course." No one was wiser than Solomon.
LORINI: The wisdom of Solomon. My own reference exactly. In my opinion, Ip . . . Copernicus should be jailed immediately.
CACCINI: Perhaps he should have been. But now we can only restrain those who share his views.
DELLE COLOMBE: Galileo is no fool. He debates philosophy, never Scripture.

CACCINI: He has had no challenge from Scripture. (*pausing*) I am to give the Christmas sermon at Santa Maria Novella.
MAGINI: You will attack Galileo? . . . on Christmas!
CACCINI: Not Galileo. Copernicus. *He* cannot answer me.
DELLE COLOMBE: Nor will Galileo defend him?
CACCINI: Perhaps not. But perhaps he will be tempted.
DELLE COLOMBE: And then . . . if he yields?
CACCINI: And then he will shatter his sword against the clouds.
DELLE COLOMBE: I have a text, a perfect text . . . The Acts of the Apostles: . . . "ye men of Galilee, why stand ye gazing up into the heavens?"

SCENE EIGHT

(*The court of Cosimo II. Present are: Cosimo II; his mother, the Grand Duchess Marina Christina; Secretary of State Cigoli; Galileo; Benedetto Castelli; and Maria Celeste.*)

CIGOLI: This attack from the pulpit, Your Serene Highness.
COSIMO: Absurd. Just another ambitious priest, obscure of birth, devoid of rank, trivial of mind, seeking a reputation on the back of fame. (*holding some documents*) Look, tributes! From half the courts of Europe. The navigator of the skies, now the prize of Tuscany.
CHRISTINA: This sermon at Maria Novella. Some friar?
CIGOLI: Father Tommaso Caccini.
CHRISTINA: I understand he attacked Signor Galileo.
CASTELLI: Too cowardly to name Galileo, he used Copernicus to shield his intent.
CHRISTINA: It concerned the earth, and also the sun, I believe. That

the one we thought to rest, moved; and that which moved was at rest . . . contrary to Holy Scripture.

(*At this moment Ciampoli enters. Galileo turns and embraces him.*)

CIAMPOLI: Cardinal Barberini asked me to bring the news. The Collegio Romano wishes to honor your discoveries with a banquet. And Prince Cesi, the most enlightened of Roman nobles, begs you to accept membership in his academy of learning. It is suggested the Holy Father may himself grant an audience.
COSIMO (*clearly elated*): A triumph for Tuscany.
CIGOLI: I urge caution, Your Highness. The armies of Europe contest the fate of Christendom. A Rome so preoccupied cannot give Professor Galileo's demonstrations fair consideration. (*turning to Galileo*) Do you agree with Copernicus, that the earth moves?
GALILEO: I believe it.
CIGOLI: Setting your will against two thousand years of philosophy.
GALILEO: Not my will, my mind. Ideas are not like wine, which improves with age. That which was wrong a thousand years ago is equally false today.
CIGOLI: Did your magical telescope see some movement of the earth?
GALILEO: I accept the demonstration of Copernicus because it is beautiful.
CIGOLI: So is that painting (*He points to the Botticelli, which has not been removed.*)
GALILEO: A different beauty, not of the senses. A beauty which is the form of truth whose symmetries disclose the laws by which He governs the world.
CIGOLI: What need has God for laws?
GALILEO: He uses them . . . look. (*He takes a transparent glass sphere from his pocket.*) After the great flood, God promised Noah never

again to destroy the race of man. The rainbow was to be token of this pledge. (*Galileo walks to the window. A shaft of white light falls upon the sphere and appears on the opposing white wall divided into all the colors of the spectrum. There is the silence of amazed attention.*) In the same manner every falling raindrop divides light from the returning sun. Through properties bestowed on nature, God renews His covenant.

COSIMO: Bravo, Galileo. The magician of Tuscany.

MARIA CELESTE (*crossing herself*): "And so our souls have sight of that immortal sea which brought us thither."

CHRISTINA: The priest was clear. That this business contradicted Scripture.

GALILEO: There is no contradiction. The Scriptures instruct us how to go to heaven, not how heaven goes. If the Scriptures seem to contradict the more precise terms of geometry, it is a difficulty of interpretation which our scholars can reconcile.

COSIMO (*to Galileo*): You hesitate. Have your austere pursuits purged your mind of the desire for honor?

GALILEO: Desire honor? I crave honor. I deserve honor. I have uncovered territories of knowledge whose very existence was unsuspected. Yet my works and name are known to a handful, while all Europe bends to the dusty copyings of charlatans.

COSIMO: Then go. Receive your honors and undeceive the world.

GALILEO: My discoveries are valuable, but I fear their outward glories may blind men to their meaning.

CIGOLI: Are you not content to revise the maps of planets? Would you reconstruct the world?

GALILEO: I come to teach men to unriddle the book of nature for themselves.

MARIA CELESTE (*surprising everyone, even herself, with her intervention*): Surely, He who attends the falling sparrow will guard the threatened eagle. A month ago, my sister Arcangela was suffering so from the cold, it seemed her frail body might shake so violently as to dislodge her spirit. The convent had no money for warm clothes and medicines, not even a coverlet for her bed. We could only pray. (*passionately*) God heard our prayers. The prayers of the voiceless poor. And He answered them, through a benefactor still unknown.

GALILEO (*to himself*): The time is ripe. (*louder*) I will go to Rome. (*aside to Castelli and Ciampoli*) First, I must dispose of this attack from the pulpit.

CIAMPOLI: It might be best to ignore disputes of Scripture.

GALILEO: I would prefer it. But my enemies are behind the mouthings of this monk. Unable to deny my reasoning, they wish to strangle my brain with false interpretations of Holy Writ.

CASTELLI: How will you answer? A commentary on Scripture?

GALILEO: Nothing public. I am not so foolish. No . . . not a book . . . a letter, to the Grand Duchess, whose piety is renowned . . . a private letter, unpublished, and thus free from the scrutiny of priestly bureaucrats.

MARIA CELESTE: I do not know those in high places, as you do. Surely those who govern the Church will know the piety of your intent.

GALILEO: First to pen, and then to coach.

CIGOLI (*to nobody in particular*): This is no time to go to Rome to talk about the moon.

SCENE NINE

(*We are returned to the sitting room of Ludovici delle Colombe. Delle Colombe again stands, facing Caccini, who is slouched in the chair, his body tensed almost as if seeking an impossible concealment, his characteristic posture.*)

DELLE COLOMBE: The arrogance! His letter to the Grand Duchess! He rewrites Holy Scripture to fit his philosophy.
CACCINI (*very mildly*): It has the ring of heresy.
DELLE COLOMBE (*impatiently*): That's your field. I am only a philosopher.

(*There is a long silence, during which the men look at each other, then begin to smile.*)

DELLE COLOMBE: Astonishing. How eagerly he embraced the snare. He seemed so politic. Perhaps he has gone mad.
CACCINI: He was not reckless . . . not wholly. It is not for circulation, but a private letter, between friends, exempt from scrutiny by the Holy Office.
DELLE COLOMBE: Not circulate! It is everywhere.

(*Lorini enters holding his own copy of the letter to the Grand Duchess.*)

LORINI: Did you see this? It's insulting. I, the country's senior professor of ecclesiastical history. I was not even consulted. Aquinas. He seems to know Aquinas. But other authorities, most weighty authorities, are wholly neglected. Didacus . . . Stunica . . . Stunica devotes a hundred pages to this same passage from Joshua. And Cusanus. How can one describe the universe without a single reference to the sainted Nicholas of Cusa, not one?
CACCINI: He is no student of Scripture.
LORINI: I will expose his errors.
CACCINI: If you descend to debate—a man of your repute—you would only affirm his right to discuss Scripture.
LORINI: He is not even ordained.
CACCINI: And this letter is not all. An acquaintance of mine overheard two disciples of the Galileist creed debating the miracles of

the saints. Were they really miracles? And was God a sensible creature, who could laugh and weep like you and me?
LORINI: The authorities will never allow this to continue.
CACCINI: If they knew.
DELLE COLOMBE: He has kept Rome in ignorance. He says everything, argues anything, but publishes nothing.
CACCINI: I would go to Rome myself. But you, Father Lorini, are the senior among us, not only in years and rank but in wisdom and in the regard of the cardinals.
DELLE COLOMBE: Well and humbly spoken, Father Caccini. Rome is a giant. Not everyone can wake a giant.
LORINI (*suitably puffed up*): Well, gentlemen, what do you suggest?
CACCINI: A direct communication.
LORINI: A communication. Excellent. Just the thing . . . but to whom?
CACCINI: To the body charged with such matters. To the Holy Inquisition.

(*There is a startled, fearful silence.*)

LORINI: The Inquisition!
CACCINI: It is their jurisdiction. The Holy Father has imposed the most solemn obligation to inform the Inquisition of the slightest hint of heresy.
LORINI: Heresy! I didn't say heresy.
DELLE COLOMBE: Nor I. I act only for the truth of philosophy.
CACCINI: Nor did I. It is not for us . . . any of us. We are bound to inform. If there is an offense, others will decide. We have no responsibility. Nor can we be revealed. Any testimony would be sealed under the secrecy of the Inquisition. Forever.
LORINI: I shall write a letter.
CACCINI: The Holy Office demands a certain precision of statement.

DELLE COLOMBE: No one is more precise than Father Lorini. Yet perhaps Father Caccini, as he just came from Rome, might be helpful with technicalities.
CACCINI: Unnecessary. (*turns to Lorini*) But, of course, if you wish.
LORINI: My scholarly labors have left little time for trivial correspondence with Roman functionaries. I would be glad to consult Father Caccini. (*pauses*) But once they receive my letter, I may be summoned to Rome. They'll want to ask questions.
CACCINI: It is customary. Should they, I would be grateful to serve as your assistant.
LORINI: I should have an assistant. (*pauses*) They may want to question you, too.
CACCINI: They may.

SCENE TEN

(*Stage darkens. The only voice heard is that of Lorenzo Seghizi, Commissary-General of the Inquisition.*)

SEGHIZI: Father Caccini, Father Lorini, we thank you for bringing these matters to our attention and for your pious submission to interrogation. You may leave us to our deliberations, remembering that you are commanded to secrecy on pain of imprisonment and excommunication. (*There is a shuffling of chairs, footsteps, silence— the sounds of men departing. Seghizi, continuing, to himself*) Conversations between unidentified men, anonymous eavesdroppers. Gossip, just gossip. "God cries!" And a private letter to a holy father who helps supervise the fortifications of the Papal States.

This is no ordinary man, this Galileo. He is the personal philosopher of the Grand Duke. Galileo himself is to be received by His Holiness. His discoveries have been applauded in every corner of the Empire. One does not strike at such a man with swords of paper. Still, Cardinal Bellarmine has asked a few questions about Galileo, curious, not accusing. The man is a philosopher, a great philosopher. He should not have involved himself with Scripture. But thought is needed, much thought; others consulted. In time it may all die away. Put these papers in Galileo's file. We shall meditate patiently until the Divine will chooses to manifest itself. (*His voice changes, deepens, becomes reverberant.*) As Commissary-General of the Congregation of the Holy Office, by the mercy of God, Cardinals of the Holy Roman Church, Inquisitors-General throughout the Christian commonwealth against heretical depravity—I bring this session to a close.

SCENE ELEVEN

(*Two soldiers sit in front of the closed curtain, wearing grimy mud-stained uniforms of the imperial army. They are surrounded by piles of books, which they are sluggishly packing into wooden crates.*)

FIRST SOLDIER: Shit!
SECOND SOLDIER: What?
FIRST SOLDIER: Shit, I said. Shit! (*Second Soldier looks uncomprehending.*) Can't you hear?

(*From behind the curtain can be heard muted sounds of subdued brawling, an occasional woman's scream, laughter of both men and women, breaking glass.*)

FIRST SOLDIER: The golden harmonies of plunder. Our comrades feast on gold and pewter, silver plate, wine, and the fat-thighed women of Nuremberg. And what are we doing?

SECOND SOLDIER: Packing books.

FIRST SOLDIER: Brilliantly put.

SECOND SOLDIER: A pious task. To thank the Pope for our victory he is sent the great library of Nuremberg.

FIRST SOLDIER: Why us? We dragged through the mud, contributed to the heap of corpses, exposed our bodies to the sword, chased the Protestants from the field. Now we forfeit our reward for his.

SECOND SOLDIER: Someone had to do it.

FIRST SOLDIER: When we finish there will be nothing but broken pewter and grandmothers. I have never seen so many books. (*He picks up a heavy volume and blows a heavy cloud of dust from the cover.*) It seems Nuremberg has more books than scholars. (*pauses*) There was one man, reading at a table, where we came in.

SECOND SOLDIER: Where did he go?

FIRST SOLDIER: I cut off his head.

SECOND SOLDIER: Was he a Protestant?

FIRST SOLDIER: He didn't say.

SECOND SOLDIER: There will be other cities to plunder.

FIRST SOLDIER: Soon Europe will not contain a single Protestant kingdom. We will be consigned to shivering watch along the icy Baltic.

SECOND SOLDIER: There are still enemy armies.

FIRST SOLDIER: Not many. And not for long. Catholics are better fighters. We are more accustomed to discipline.

SECOND SOLDIER: There are Protestant rulers beyond the Baltic.

FIRST SOLDIER: Swedes, Norwegians. Not Protestants . . . pagans, barbarians . . . Turks. We redeem Christians, not savages. We cannot march the waves, and could we, to what end, to feast on snow and animal flesh? (*pausing*) The Pope has enough books. Enough of everything.

SECOND SOLDIER: Except souls. That is why we fight.

FIRST SOLDIER: We fight at the command of Spain. We fight because we prefer the risk of death in battle to certain death in prison. We fight for the spoils of victory which are now deprived us.

SECOND SOLDIER: And for the cross.

FIRST SOLDIER: The cross. Of course. For the cross. (*Holds up a battle flag on which is emblazoned a cross on the Hapsburg coat of arms.*) Look. A cross. A Spanish cross. We have thousands like it . . . in Spain.

SECOND SOLDIER: It is also the cross of Rome.

FIRST SOLDIER: I saw no Italians on the battlefield.

SECOND SOLDIER: You are a Catholic.

FIRST SOLDIER: Like many, I was born a Catholic. Unlike some, I have earned my faith with these arms. I am a Spaniard. One can be both Catholic and Spaniard.

SECOND SOLDIER: Your anger tempts you toward sacrilege.

FIRST SOLDIER (*standing, shouting*): I am not angry! (*throwing book to the floor, sitting down, pauses, then quietly*) It is difficult to serve two masters in one day.

SECOND SOLDIER: Rome will be generous. They may reward us.

FIRST SOLDIER: With a *Te deum* if we live and a mass if we perish.

SECOND SOLDIER: You share in the glory. That cannot be taken away. We restore the universal Church.

FIRST SOLDIER: That is of concern to kings, emperors, and popes. I must provide for my family.

SECOND SOLDIER: When the war is over—

FIRST SOLDIER: We will be very poor. (*He throws more books on floor and begins to leave.*)

SECOND SOLDIER: You will be shot.

FIRST SOLDIER: Now or later, but at least with wine in my belly.

(*The lights go down, soldiers and props are removed, and the curtain opens.*)

Note to Scene Twelve

Galileo goes to Rome and, as we shall see, displays his brilliance in the leading salons of that sophisticated, corrupt, cynical city—which is also the guardian of the Church and, more important, of hopes for the renaissance of the Church.

In the upper ranks of Christendom, the Counter-Reformation—vigorous, austere, pitiless—is in full control, its baroque spirit essentially hostile to that of the lavish, libertine, incandescent Renaissance. Galileo and his friends are the last of the Renaissance men, living in the misguided belief that the ambience that allowed Michelangelo and Leonardo da Vinci to come to fruition still encompasses them. Galileo—an accomplished musician, writer, and craftsman—embodies the expansiveness of a dying age, and is also among the first of the moderns. His work proclaims the onset of mathematical experimental thought, with its claim to supreme validity in an ever widening sphere, whereas those who confront him, garbed in what appears to be the fresh voice of a reformed Church, are the hopeless defenders of an obsolete and doomed idea—that of the universal Church with supreme spiritual and, even, an ultimate temporal authority.

From our own century, we can understand that each was very different than they then appeared to be to themselves and to others. The Emperor and the Pope were deadly enemies, although they shared the same obsolete, obsessive vision. Richelieu and Galileo were strangers, yet they brought the new world—that of science, reason, and the nation-state—to birth. Richelieu and the Pope were allies, and they won their war, but the victory cost the Church its world. The agonies of emergence were the most prolonged, violent, bloody, and pitiless that Europe was to endure for three hundred years—until, that is, our own time.

Galileo's expressed motive for going to Rome is to answer and halt the allegations that he and his doctrines are contrary to Scripture, theology, etc. He cannot respond in his usual manner—that is, through published polemical refutations—because that would be far too dangerous for anyone not an established theologian. It might even be heresy. Nor is it likely that the somewhat hostile Dominicans and Jesuits would allow such a book to receive the imprimatur. Yet the attacks on him have not been serious. (He does not know of the Inquisition hearings and, in any event, those hearings came to very little beyond a kind of yellow light.) They consist of Caccini's sermons, the muttering of some monks and professors in Florence, and rumors from Rome—transmitted to him by friends—that there is some hostile gossip, none of it traceable to the ruling echelons of the hierarchy. Although men friendly to him—Castelli, Ciampoli, Barberini, Cesi—think that his presence in Rome might help to squelch the hostile gossip and implications, they know there are some risks. On balance, they would advise him to say nothing more than he had in his letters, be quiet for a while, and let the dispute and discussion simply evaporate. (One must remember that none of them know of the secret Inquisition proceedings. Had they, they would have urged him to stay away.)

This motive, expressed by Galileo, is in large part a pretext. He has been a convinced Copernican since his early twenties, but uncertainty and fear about the reaction of the Church have made him omit any assertion of his convictions from his works—including those most closely related to the subject. He had even ignored Kepler when that astronomer of the imperial court urged him to take a public stand—as Kepler himself had done in order to advance public acceptance of the new doctrines. Now a man in his fifties, conscious of time slipping past, Galileo looks upon the contemptible attacks not as dangers but as providing a moment of opportunity. He could not have raised the theological and scriptural issues himself, but others have done that for him. Since they have been raised, he believes he can now press to a triumphant resolution. He will go to Rome confident that the force of his arguments and reason will persuade the masters of theology to admit or decide that the word of God does not exclude the Copernican doctrine, that the latter can be adopted as a valid cosmology, describing a physical reality, without theological transgression.

This was a serious miscalculation.

At this point, circa 1616, the leaders of the Church were in no mood to consider the question that was all-important to Galileo. The Pope, Paul V, had little interest in intellectual or artistic matters. (He is supposed to have said, "Better new jobs for laborers than new ideas from philosophers.") The intellectual leader of the Church, and the most powerful of its governors, was Roberto Cardinal Bellarmine (made a saint in the 1920s). He had done much to shape the Counter-Reformation which had halted the Protestant advance. He still hoped that the Protestant heresy might be extirpated and a universal Catholic Church reestablished, with both spiritual and temporal authority.

This hope was not then as unreasonable as it might now seem. There were men still living in Rome who had witnessed Protestant and Catholic churches convene peacefully in Regensburg in search of that Christian unity which was, to their minds, the natural and desirable order of things. The breakdown of this meeting—over two irreconcilable differences of doctrine—ended hopes of peaceful accommodation, but it did not make the Church yield its claim or diminish its aspirations to universal dominion.

It was clear by 1616 that the time of opportunity and danger for the Church and for the states of Europe was fast approaching. The Thirty Years' War, heralded by the unprecedented comets of 1618, was less than two years away. No one could foresee that by the end of that war—and partly as its consequence—the structure of European civilization would be fundamentally altered, and forces set in motion that would influence the direction of European history for more than three centuries.

In 1616, the leading Catholic powers were Spain, France, Poland, and much of Germany. Protestantism or, more exactly, varying types of non-Catholic Christianity were ascendant in England, Scandinavia, and parts of Germany. This use of national names is a convenience of description, for the nation-state as we now know it did not exist. Monarchs presided over confederations of lesser nobles—dukes, barons, princes—who held many important aspects of sovereign power over their own chunks of European soil. This was most marked in Germany. Indeed, there was no Germany: only a grouping of relatively independent princes whose nominal lord was the Holy Roman Emperor, who kept his court in Prague.

By 1616 the goals of Catholic and Protestant German princes had become so irreconcilable that only force could settle the differences. Spain was already preparing an army to march through northern Italy and along the French border toward conquest of the Protestant Netherlands. Both Germany and France feared that Spain's ambitions might extend even further—into their own territories. Spain was already the most influential foreign power in Italy. Indeed, Spain actually controlled some parts of the Italian peninsula, most importantly the city of Naples, south of Rome; had influence over others; and was feared by all, including the Pope. It was, after all, less than a century since the Spanish, under Emperor Charles V, had sacked Rome and made the Pope a prisoner.

The multifarious omens of war came at a time when the Emperor Matthias was visibly near termination of a noble but lingering old age. It would soon be necessary to choose a new Holy Roman Emperor, and under unprecedented conditions—by German leaders divided along religious lines. The Emperor had traditionally come from the House of Hapsburg, which also ruled Spain, still nominally part of the Empire. A militantly Catholic Emperor joined by blood to the royal house of Spain might constitute an alliance whose power could not be resisted by any grouping of other European states.

In this situation the Church of Rome had fatally inconsistent objectives. It wished to reestablish its authority throughout Europe, but that would require a Holy Roman Emperor willing to go to war for the cause. But the Church of Rome was not merely a spiritual authority. It was also a temporal state. And as such it feared the extension of Spanish power over the papal dominions. A triumphant Empire led by the military power of Spain would increase this danger. It was necessary for the Church to find a Catholic counterweight—a power that could help restore Catholicism while resisting Spanish designs on Italy. The only candidate was France—which, like the Pope, both wished a Catholic restoration and feared the power of Spain. For both Pope and France, the fear would be a stronger motivation than the wish for Catholic restoration.

Bellarmine was deeply engaged in the continual papal effort to influence oncoming events—the choice of Emperor, the realignments of power, etc. He was also principally responsible for continuing the momentum of internal change known as the Counter-Reformation. And he had recently become involved in a dispute with King James I of England—conducted by letter and by the publication of contending books—over that monarch's doctrine of the "divine right of kings." This was to prove a more dangerous and subversive doctrine than the theses of Luther or the *Institutes* of Calvin. For how could the Church claim authority over a ruler who derived his own power directly from God? Moreover, divinely granted power was obviously considered supreme over the secular authority of lesser nobles within the state. The doctrine that James defended not only challenged the supreme authority of the Church but replaced it with the supreme authority of the centralized state. Bellarmine was the better debater, but King James proved the more accurate prophet.

This, then, was hardly a time to expect the hierarchy to welcome a leisurely exploration of theological issues raised by different conceptions of the relative movements of earth and sun. Copernicus had been dead for almost a century. Since then, no scientist or mathematician had been kept from freely studying or discussing any theory of the world—whether that of Copernicus, or Ptolemy, or Tycho Brahe, or anyone else. Moreover, Copernicus, although Polish, was an honored subject of the Holy Roman Empire, and Kepler, an openly avowed Copernican, had been designated as chief astronomer to the imperial court at Prague even though he was a Protestant.

The Church was not inclined to be bothered with this issue when faced with so many more pressing problems. Moreover, any resolution would have damaging consequences. To vindicate Galileo would require a formal reinterpretation of long-established doctrine and, in consequence, would strengthen the Protestants' claim that they had the greater fidelity to Holy Writ. (Luther and Calvin had condemned Copernicus long before.) On the other hand, it would be hard to explain why Copernicus' work had not been challenged for seventy-five years. Nor did the Church wish to appear as the enemy of intellectual exploration, when its enemies were trying to arouse fears of papal absolutism with grotesquely exaggerated descriptions of papal claims to rigorous control over all forms of thought, study, and art.

But the issue was forced on the papal hierarchy, and not by the enemies and accusers of Galileo. These were, for the most part, men of little distinction, whose suspicions and charges had been carefully studied and found—if not totally untrue—hardly of sufficient weight and substance to call for intervention by the Congregation of the Holy Office. It was Galileo himself who forced the issue. He had admitted that he was a Copernican and had argued for an interpretation of Scripture that would sanction that doctrine. Admittedly, he had scrupulously observed the procedures which made it possible to categorize his opinions as, technically, private and unpublished, but they were known among educated men throughout Europe, no more so than in Rome, where the Dominicans and Jesuits vied for intellectual and theological preeminence.

By coming to Rome, Galileo implicitly informed Europe that the Church knew of his opinions. After all, he was one of the most famous men in Europe, personal philosopher to the Grand Duke of Tuscany, author of works read in every part of the civilized world. It was inevitable, therefore, that his expressed opinions and his intentions in coming to Rome would be widely communicated. To ignore this would, in fact, appear as silent acquiescence in his views. So the necessity for decision was inescapable.

That being so, there could be no doubt about the answer. Scripture had very little to say on the subject of astronomy, but on those few occasions when it did speak, it plainly asserted that the earth was the center around which the sun and planets moved. And that reading had been accepted from the beginning of scriptural exegesis. Moreover, there was no proof of Copernicus' theory—no physical, tangible proof of the kind that might persuade theologians to examine the possibility that the Bible had been misinterpreted for a thousand years. (This had happened when Magellan's crew found people living on the opposite side of the globe, a possibility also precluded, it was believed, by certain biblical passages.) And the question was not unimportant. It was a significant element in the creation of the Christian cosmology—a divine order of the universe that placed man's struggle for salvation on a plane intermediate between Hades at the center and Paradise at the boundary of the world. To accept what Galileo said, therefore, would require not only changing settled interpretations but overturning the cosmology of divine order. And for what? Not only was there no physical proof but there had been no celestial observations which could not also be explained on the model of a geocentric universe. Underneath the endless discussion was the reality that adherents of Copernicanism preferred it because it was mathematically tidier, more symmetrical, and provided slightly less complex explanations for some of the observed phenomena. But these largely aesthetic considerations, though they might interest mathematicians, had not the slightest relevance to theology.

Thus the decision on the doctrinal questions was inevitable, not even likely to stimulate serious debate. But Galileo was still a problem. His views were well known. To ignore him would seem hypocrisy or favoritism or fear. To condemn him would excite questions and debate throughout Europe, with unforeseeable consequences in the continent's volatile and precarious politics. This was not the time for a cause célèbre—like that aroused by the burning of Giordano Bruno, which Bellarmine had ordered sixteen years before.

The problem was a practical one, an affair of state.

SCENE TWELVE

(*We are in the meticulously lavish gardens surrounding the Roman villa of Prince Federigo Cesi—among the noblest of Romans, founder of the famous Lyncean Academy, and Galileo's most powerful friend in Italy. There is music, fireworks, illusions—entertainments of the kind customarily given by the great households in lavish display of their wealth and as tribute to their guests.*

(*A scattered group is gathered for discussion alongside a table of delicacies, while servants pour the wine. It includes Galileo; Ciampoli; Cardinal Maffeo Barberini; Francesco, Barberini's nephew, later to be Cardinal Francesco; Francesco Niccolini, Cosimo's Ambassador to Rome; Cigoli; Father Horatio Grassi, a professor of mathematics at the Collegio Romano; and a few unidentified noblemen.*)

NOBLEMAN: If the earth was moving, stones thrown into the air would land behind us.

(*A small cart carrying food for the guests comes by. Galileo halts it, and turns to the nobleman.*)
GALILEO: Observe. (*He picks up a stone and—with startling nimbleness for a man in his middle fifties—leaps aboard the cart. He signals the driver to go ahead, and the cart begins to move. Galileo drops the stone into the cart.*) It falls at my feet. What seemed one motion was two—drawn down by the earth and forward by the cart. Similarly, since the earth carries forward everything, we all share that motion, so we cannot see it.

(*Galileo steps off the cart somewhat clumsily, and the noblemen along with Cigoli and Father Grassi cluster around him.*)

NOBLEMAN (*to Galileo*): Since motion is the cause of heat, if the earth moved, the heat would be unbearable. Aristotle is plain on that. He explains how the ancient Babylonians cooked eggs by whirling them through the air in slings.

GALILEO: I, too, have pondered the meaning of that passage in Aristotle. Naturally, it is not permissible to doubt the accuracy of his reports. This once must have been a method of cooking eggs. But perhaps we have drawn the wrong conclusion. We can observe that for us Italians whirling an egg through the air does not cook it; indeed, it will make a hot egg cool. (*pausing*) Yet we have eggs, do we not?

OTHERS: Yes, in plenty.

GALILEO: We have slings to hold them?

OTHERS: Agreed.

GALILEO: Nor do we lack strong young men to whirl the slings?

OTHERS: True.

GALILEO: Yet the eggs do not cook.

OTHERS (*murmuring*): No, not at all.

GALILEO: How, then, can we explain Aristotle's observation? (*silence*) We lack only one element of Aristotle's illustration. We are not Babylonians. It is being Babylonians, therefore, not motion, that causes the cooking of the eggs.

(*Galileo's friends, even Cardinal Barberini, laugh—but not the questioner or Father Grassi. Cigoli seems disconcerted with the display.*)

CIGOLI (*whispering to Galileo*): When you make men fools, you make them enemies.

GRASSI: And what of the prophets? Ecclesiastes tells us, "The sun also ariseth, and the sun goeth down, and hasteth to his place where he arose."

(*The atmosphere of lively dispute and inoffensive wit dissolves. There is an uneasy silence.*)

GALILEO (*showing an unaccustomed touch of timidity*): I admit the force of the passage. But Scripture can be imperfectly understood. (*The group becomes visibly uneasy.*)
BARBERINI (*walking up and lightly touching Galileo on the arm*): If our learned guests will forgive me, I have some private communications for Signor Galileo.

(*All seem relieved and break up into smaller groups.*)

BARBERINI: Confine your debate to science, my dear friend.
GALILEO: I would, but I am forced to other ground—
BARBERINI (*interrupting*): Once you begin to talk about Scripture, you only encourage a host of fools. They will ask, if the earth is not at the center, where does the devil live? Or, if we are only a planet like other planets, what of Adam and Eve, and the great flood? Did they happen on every world? You can see the morass which lies in that direction.
GALILEO: How can I describe the world if it is maintained that Scripture forbids its description?
BARBERINI: Scripture sets no limit to thought. If we could better understand events or navigate with greater accuracy by assuming the world to be square, why then we can call it a square. As long as we do not insist that it actually is a square.
GALILEO: The ice . . . you remember, at my home, in Venice.
BARBERINI: A remarkable display.
GALILEO: The Church . . . I speak hypothetically, you understand . . . could find scriptural justification for the weight of ice. It could command the faithful to believe ice heavier than water. But it could not make the ice sink.
BARBERINI: Not unless a priest were assigned to hold it down. We do not disagree. Should a scriptural reading contradict observation, we must uncover the source of error.

GALILEO: To find the truth?
BARBERINI: To sustain the faith. To maintain what ordinary perception denies is a temptation to disobedience. Nevertheless, our senses are fallible. There is what we see and what is. Are they the same? Perhaps. But certainty is forever hidden by our mortality. A quality you share, do you not, Galileo?
GALILEO: And suppose—I speak hypothetically of course—our senses should provide proof of a circling earth centered on an immobile sun?
BARBERINI: We should most carefully reexamine our reading. But we have no such proof.
GALILEO: If—
BARBERINI: Nor shall we. There are many ways to knowledge— the brush of Michelangelo, the navigation of Columbus, Bernini's marble, Galileo's geometry. All ennoble the race of man. Then, there is God's knowledge. Set apart from our own. The mystery of the world is the mystery of God Himself. Within that mystery is the Divine ocean from which flow the glistening springs of faith.
GALILEO: Are we forbidden to pursue the discoveries of Copernicus?
BARBERINI (*in a lighter tone*): Of course not. Copernicus himself advised Pope Gregory's revision of the calendar. His value to the Church did not require us to accept his universe. Men are not forbidden to think, or to contrive novel theories, if they recognize the limitations as well as the gifts God has bestowed. One day your philosophy may illuminate the world. But it cannot receive just consideration in this Rome so embroiled in the present tumult of bloody restoration.
GALILEO (*half to himself*): The time. It is not ours to choose.

(*As the two men part and Galileo leaves, Barberini is approached hurriedly by an agitated Ciampoli.*)

CIAMPOLI: Cardinal Bellarmine has requested our appearance. It may concern Galileo.

(*A bell begins to ring from St. Peter's. Its tones are quickly echoed by other church bells from all parts of Rome until the city shimmers in a crescendo of sound. There is a loud, acclaiming shout from the guests in other parts of the garden.*)

CIAMPOLI: Nuremberg has fallen.
BARBERINI: Another imperial victory.
CIAMPOLI: Yet the fears of Richelieu remain a fantasy.
BARBERINI: Thus far . . . (*pauses*) with Bellarmine we must be cautious.
CIAMPOLI: Galileo has done nothing.
BARBERINI: Of course not. Yet I suspect he has enemies among the Jesuits.
CIAMPOLI: There is a Jesuit priest in the tent of every Spanish general.
BARBERINI: Their view is ascendant. We would not awake any suspicion that my service as ambassador inclines me to France.
CIAMPOLI: You served at the Pope's command.
BARBERINI: We know that. But service and sympathy are easily confused. The next Council will be divided and cannot select one thought partisan to any Catholic power.
CIAMPOLI: You are partisan only to the Church.
BARBERINI: Truth is not enough. Appearance is of equal weight. Let us go. A request from Cardinal Bellarmine cannot be ignored.

SCENE THIRTEEN

(*A spacious office overlooking a walled Vatican courtyard. Paneled in Italian chestnut of rare figure, interrupted only by delicately carpentered doors and framed windows of Venetian glass, the interior of the room is surprisingly austere. The floors are bare and the walls undecorated by paintings or tapestries. The only furniture consists of a single wooden chair for visitors; a flat undistinguished worktable, on which are piled a handful of books; and a chair and large desk, equally plain, on which we see a single, neat stack of documents. Seated at the desk is Roberto Cardinal Bellarmine, the unchallenged authority over Catholic theology. Facing him are Ciampoli and Cardinal Barberini. They are standing, not out of deference or obedience to protocol, but because there is only one chair. Cardinal Bellarmine does not seem to notice the shortage of seats. The bells of Rome continue to ring.*)

BELLARMINE (*musing*): The psalms say of the sun, "It rejoiceth like a giant in running his course." I once became curious to know how long it took the sun to set at sea. While visiting a friend's seaside villa in Spoleto, I began to recite the psalm "Miserere" as the sun began its descent. And before I had read it twice over, the sun was gone. It must have been that in so short a time the sun had run more than the space of seven thousand miles. Who could have believed so enormous a motion, had reason not demonstrated it?

CIAMPOLI: I was not aware that Your Eminence took an interest in scientific questions.

BELLARMINE: A man of bookish temperament, like myself, is not wholly exempt from curiosity about the displays of nature.

CIAMPOLI: On the matter of Galileo.

BELLARMINE: He has resurrected this annoying question of the movement of sun and earth.

BARBERINI: An issue for mathematicians.

BELLARMINE: We have always supposed it so, Maffeo. Unfortunately, it has been forced upon us. A Carmelite friar in Naples, one Foscarini, has written a treatise presuming to interpret Scripture as support for the Copernican theory. Your Galileo has not helped matters.

CIAMPOLI: He has written nothing in support of the Copernican doctrine. Nor has he debated Scripture except in private letters and, occasionally, in private discussions.

BELLARMINE: *Private* discussions, you say, *private* letters. So private they are talked about in every household of Rome. The man is everywhere—at every dinner, at every entertainment. I am told there is no way to escape his grasp. Nor can any contend with him. He turns men's arguments into jokes, lures them into logical traps. One might almost think he hoped to compel this mighty globe itself to move with the incredible energy of his own argument. As for his personal letters . . . *they* have provided employment for a hundred copyists.

BARBERINI: Like me, he is a son of Florence. There, it is more common to discuss intellectual and artistic questions with outward passion than is the case in Rome.

BELLARMINE: Then he should have remained in Florence. I have observed the swiftness of your rise, Maffeo. The Italian cardinal who baptized the King of France while retaining the friendship of the Spanish bishops has demonstrated that even a man of Florence can master his turbulent heritage. (*pauses*) The Holy Father had no choice except to refer the matter to the Qualifiers of the Holy Office.

(*From the shadowed area behind Cardinal Barberini steps a robed and hooded man—a Dominican of the Inquisition—"the black-and-white hounds of the Lord." Others behind him are perceptible only as shapes in the shadows. His voice, if not that of Father Seghizi, is remarkably similar to it.*)

DOMINICAN (*holding a parchment, his features obscured by his hood, reading*): The first of the two propositions holds that the sun is the center of the world. We find this proposition foolish and absurd philosophically, and formally heretical, inasmuch as it contradicts the doctrine of the Holy Scripture.

The second proposition holds that the earth is not the center of the world nor immovable, but moves according to the whole of itself. We find this proposition to receive the same censure in philosophy and, as regards theological truth, to be at least erroneous in faith.

(*The figure steps back into darkness.*)

BARBERINI (*slowly, cautiously*): A most weighty opinion. But only an opinion. It does not make the Copernican doctrine a formal heresy. (*Bellarmine nods in seeming acquiescence.*)
CIAMPOLI (*agitated*): It warns any mathematician that he risks heresy.
BELLARMINE (*losing his calm and friendly demeanor*): Mathematics! Are we all to bow before mathematics? Mathematics are for mathematicians, forbidden to contradict the judgments of theology. Lesser ways to knowledge must yield to greater. God has so ordered the world. (*He continues in a more formal tone.*) Having considered the opinions of his advisers, the Holy Father has decided to prohibit the works of Foscarini and all other works which pretend to conform Scripture with the principles of Copernicus. As for Copernicus himself, his work is simply suspended, pending correction. These corrections are trivial—a few words, an occasional phrase that might cause the false impression that Copernicus wrote other than hypothetically.
CIAMPOLI: What of Galileo?
BELLARMINE: He has disturbed the faith.

BARBERINI (*tentatively*): He is only a philosopher of nature. Philosophy has nothing to do with faith.

BELLARMINE: For more years than any of us will see, the bones of Copernicus have been left untouched. He has been remembered, if at all, as a man of simple piety and great learning. Now comes this Galileo, explorer of the universe, the most illustrious scientist of the age, chief philosopher to His Most Serene Highness the Grand Duke of Tuscany. Now comes this Galileo! Fortified with all these honors—given him for what?—for building a toy! (*Barberini holds up the telescope which has been standing on a pedestal beside his desk.*) And for having the wit, or the luck, to point it at the stars while other men were looking into the windows of their neighbors. Now comes this Galileo! This most illustrious jewel in the crown of Tuscany—why? To show us some wondrous discovery, perhaps? Or some ingenious and valuable instrument crafted in his workroom? No—not for that does he come. He comes to Rome . . . the seat of Peter . . . the center of the faith . . . the home of those charged by God Himself to guard the holy wisdom—(*pauses*) He comes to counsel us on the meaning of Scripture.

He will have us—the Holy Church—provide holy sanction for the astonishing claim that his science is not only useful, not only new, not only brilliant, but unveils the truth of Divine Creation. We are to liberate Galileo so he can limit the possibilities of God. (*There is silence. The others stand, waiting for the uncharacteristic tone of angry passion to subside. The Cardinal visibly relaxes, sits back in his chair, replaces the telescope, almost smiles.*)

CIAMPOLI: None of Galileo's works contains so extravagant a claim.

BELLARMINE: True enough, Giovanni, he has been most circumspect. Had it been otherwise, he might even now be stretched in the lowest chambers of that building—there (*points through a window*), his body in the hands of men who inherit centuries of ac-

cumulated knowledge in the uses of pain. (*pauses*) Nevertheless, we all know he believes it to be true. And he is not the only one.
BARBERINI: His enemies abused the Scriptures to attack him. He was a fool to answer.
BELLARMINE: A famous fool. The most famous in Europe. It is his fame, not his foolishness, that makes him dangerous.
BARBERINI: And argues most strongly for mildness in rebuke.
BELLARMINE: Do you intervene for this man?
BARBERINI: Of course not. The affair is beyond my jurisdiction. My only concern is with the Church. It would not do well to deal harshly with this man. To destroy him now would challenge the piety of every ruler who has praised his work and entreated his assistance.
BELLARMINE: They would yield to the judgment of the Church.
BARBERINI: Certainly. But the judgment would be questioned, explanation required, disputatious doubts incited, just when the Church is most in need of obedient support. Many will not understand—to honor a man and then condemn him. It would arouse distrust, not of the faith but of the intentions of authority so newly and precariously won.
BELLARMINE: We cannot ignore him. We cannot permit every man with an idea—genius or lunatic—to justify himself through Scripture. We ourselves would not have chosen the doctrines of Copernicus for this confrontation, but it has been forced upon us, my dear Giovanni, by your zealous and insistent Galileo.
BARBERINI: In religious matters he is an obedient Catholic.
BELLARMINE: I shall consider my decision. (*He rises and leaves the room.*)
CIAMPOLI: A terrible blow. Copernicus contrary to Scripture! And the scientific reasons he thought irresistible . . . dismissed even without a hearing.
BARBERINI: Scientific reasons! Did you suppose the cardinals of the Congregation would sit to debate problems of geometry? Man does

not reason his way to heaven. (*pausing reflectively*) Had it been my decision, I would not have asked for a formal opinion. It was a mistake, on all sides of the dispute, to resort to Scripture like some pack of Lutherans. We cannot raise every academic dispute to a question of theology.

(*Bellarmine reenters, silently resumes the seat behind his desk, pauses, as if enjoying the suspense, then speaks.*)

BELLARMINE: At the direction of the Holy Father, I have summoned Galileo. I am to inform Galileo of the opinion of the Qualifiers and direct him to abandon the opinion that the sun is the center of the world around which the earth revolves.
CIAMPOLI: He may discuss the doctrine but not believe it.
BELLARMINE: Exactly.
CIAMPOLI: There is to be no public—
BELLARMINE: There will be no public proceedings, no condemnation, no penance, no recantation. Only a minute of this procedure to be placed in the secret files of the Inquisition. It is the least that can be done. I assume he will agree to abandon the opinion. I hope so. For should Galileo refuse to acquiesce, the Holy Father has ordered the Commissary-General to serve a formal injunction that would prohibit him from teaching or discussing the Copernican doctrine in any way whatsoever, an injunction whose violation would subject him to the treatment received by a relapsed heretic. I trust this further step—which would forbid Galileo from even hypothetical discussion and cloud his entire reputation—will not be necessary. But you should know there are some who do not share this hope. (*pauses, then, with the customary courtesy of dismissal*) We are grateful for your assistance. (*Barberini and Ciampoli start to leave.*) Ah, Maffeo, men are so like frogs. They go openmouthed for the lure of things which do not concern them,

and that wily angler the devil knows how to capture multitudes of them.

BARBERINI (*turning to Ciampoli as they leave*): You are not allowed to reveal this judgment to Galileo. But you are his friend. Tell him he does not come to debate. He must acquiesce in everything that is asked, without argument or question. Any other course would involve him in great peril. And he must immediately return to Florence, depart this city, where traps are found on every corner. (*Ciampoli starts to speak, but Barberini goes on.*) You can still reach him before he goes to Bellarmine. And remember, Giovanni, although the stakes are highest for Galileo, the wisdom of my counsel is also being tested. I will take a walk in the garden. The sun is beginning to set, and there will be a wonderful view of the evening star . . . (*laughing*) if it is a star.

SCENE FOURTEEN

(*Later that evening. Cardinal Bellarmine is seated in his office with Commissary-General Seghizi, Father Caccini, and Father Grassi. The Commissary-General is talking.*)

BELLARMINE: You understand, Seghizi: there will be no public proceedings, no repentance. Should he agree to abandon the Copernican doctrine, the injunction will not be issued.
SEGHIZI (*indicating paper*): I do. But the procedure is quite unusual. If no injunction is issued, there will be no lawful basis for prosecution should he later demonstrate such beliefs.
CACCINI (*breaking in*): Quite right, my lord. A man can be punished for heresy or for violating a formal injunction, but not for changing his mind.

(*Bellarmine turns toward Caccini as if noticing him for the first time. His demeanor exhibits curiosity and contempt—more of the latter.*)

BELLARMINE: This Galileo, Father, has he offended you?
CACCINI: I have no personal enmity toward the man. I scarcely know him. It is a matter of conscience.
BELLARMINE: Your conscience has carried you a long way. Are you now to be employed in the regulation of ecclesiastical procedures?
CACCINI: Oh no, my lord. I have not been trained in the law.
BELLARMINE: Strange, I would have thought you a scholar in such matters.

(*Caccini, having been thoroughly disposed of, has lost the arrogant confidence with which he entered. Confused, and a little fearful, he slowly inches to the rear of the little group.*)

BELLARMINE (*addressing himself to Seghizi*): As always, your knowledge of the law is faultless. But this is an unusual case. The Holy Father does not wish to try Galileo or to interfere with discussions of natural philosophy. The present action is only a warning. (*more sternly*) Should Galileo refuse my directions, then you will issue the injunction immediately. It is prepared? (*The Commissary-General nods, showing a parchment with a large red seal.*)
CACCINI (*aside*): The man cannot cease to believe what he believes. It is not in his nature.

(*All except Bellarmine retire to a small anteroom, leaving the door between open. They will be able to hear what is said but can be seen only as shadowed figures. Galileo will glimpse their shapes during his meeting, adding to his sense of dread and to the ominous tone of this encounter, which even Bellarmine's amiability cannot suppress. Bellarmine goes to the closet, dons his robe, then his biretta, returns to his desk, and signals the guard. As Galileo enters, Bellarmine rises to greet him, shows him to the seat facing the desk, and resumes his own chair.)*

BELLARMINE: I have, of course, heard much of you, Signor Galileo. I regret our first meeting takes place under such—shall we say—difficult conditions.
GALILEO: You are kind.
BELLARMINE *(half to himself)*: It is no kindness to prolong this. *(in more direct and somber tones)* Some time ago the Holy Father submitted certain propositions from the theories of Copernicus to the Qualifiers of the Holy Office. Here are their conclusions.

(He hands the paper to Galileo, who reads slowly, his face evidencing increasing despair. Galileo hands the paper back.)

GALILEO: Will this be published?
BELLARMINE: There is no cause. It is an advisory opinion, an internal document of the Church. *(pauses)* You understand it fully?
GALILEO: Yes, Your Eminence.
BELLARMINE: Good. *(reads from another document)* I have been instructed by the Holy Father to admonish you, Galileo Galilei of Florence, to abandon the doctrine of Copernicus that the sun is the center of the world and immovable, and that the earth is not the center of the world but moves around the sun and also on its own motion. *(He looks up.)* Do you agree to abandon this opinion?
GALILEO: I remain obedient to the will of the Church.

(Bellarmine relaxes. He is clearly pleased and relieved. Galileo is still sitting tensely, as if waiting for the ax to fall. Only gradually does he realize that the formal proceeding is over.)

BELLARMINE: You may return to Florence, where you will continue to bless us with the fruits of your genius. (*He starts as if to rise, when Galileo speaks.*)
GALILEO: May I make a request of Your Eminence?
BELLARMINE: Please.
GALILEO: I have enemies in both Rome and Florence. They may rumor that some personal penalty has been imposed upon me. If Your Excellency could give me a letter, in your own hand, stating the true nature of this procedure, it would silence such false accusations.
BELLARMINE: Gladly. (*He begins to write, mumbling.*) Signor Galileo has agreed to abandon his opinion. No penance . . . not asked to recant or abjure in any way . . . Done under my hand and seal, et cetera. Roberto Cardinal Bellarmine. (*He hands over letter.*)
GALILEO: I am grateful.

(*Cardinal Bellarmine rises, as does Galileo, who departs. Bellarmine sits down at his desk again, humming, then suddenly remembers the men waiting in the anteroom and motions them to reenter.*)

BELLARMINE (*speaking directly to Seghizi*): Simple enough. Place a minute of this meeting in Galileo's file.
SEGHIZI: Yes, Your Eminence.
BELLARMINE: The injunction? (*Seghizi holds up the parchment.*) Destroy it.
CACCINI (*reaching for document*): I will do it for you, Your Excellency.

(*Seghizi absentmindedly hands over the document. Bellarmine stands—a gesture of dismissal.*)

SCENE FIFTEEN

(*A few weeks later. Florence. A small anteroom adjoining the throne room of the Grand Duke. Present are Castelli and Maria Celeste, who is now about twenty years old. The luxuriously carpeted room contains a settee and two chairs, plush and richly embroidered in green. Above the couch is a large portrait of Lorenzo de' Medici. The windows look toward the hills of Florence.*)

CASTELLI: Shall we risk the greatest mind in Christendom?
MARIA CELESTE: There is no danger. He was not punished.
CASTELLI: He has been warned.
MARIA CELESTE: Not to silence.
CASTELLI: To the danger of speech.
MARIA CELESTE: His philosophy is his life. Will you encourage him to flee from shadow dangers to certain extinction?
CASTELLI: It is for him to decide. The risk is his alone.
MARIA CELESTE: It is also mine.
CASTELLI: You have your own vocation.
MARIA CELESTE: He is my vocation. My father and my God. I serve them both.
CASTELLI: Equally!
MARIA CELESTE: As one. (*pauses*) In the convent cells, every woman has fixed a picture of their patron saint. All save one. I have only a sketch of my father hung beside the crucifixion of Our Lord.
CASTELLI: You pray to Galileo?
MARIA CELESTE: Not to him. Not for him. Before him. As solitary witness to my faith.
CASTELLI: Your faith needs no witness.
MARIA CELESTE: My father confined me to convent life when I was a child of thirteen. For the sake of his work, I was denied the sustenance of family, the gaieties of youth, the warmth of a companioned bed.

CASTELLI: To better serve the Church of Christ.

MARIA CELESTE: There are many ways to serve. Like you, Benedetto, who are also free to explore the myriad world.

CASTELLI: Are you angry at your father?

MARIA CELESTE: No longer. I came to know him as a man of generous love, who could not have done this thing unless moved by a higher will. I learned to accept, knowing that God had chosen my father's mind as His instrument to serve His Holy Church, to whose service I was betrothed. We were linked in God's compelled denial. To renounce this service now would hollow all our years of painful strife.

CASTELLI: They cannot be relived. He has no obligation to sacrifice what remains?

MARIA CELESTE: He is obliged to God, who has made him the vessel of new truth. To refuse so terrible and rare a gift would shatter the soul into dust finer than the embers of the Inquisition.

CASTELLI: He cannot continue alone. And who now will dare to assist him?

MARIA CELESTE: We will, Benedetto. I will prepare correspondence and manuscripts. You can keep him from jealous clerics and professors. Our protection will liberate the hours for his solitary explorations.

CASTELLI: Would you even help him defy the Church?

MARIA CELESTE: He does not defy. He will succeed. And the justice of the Church will enfold him.

CASTELLI: The Church is just in spirit, but powerful in body. Justice has eternity for correction. No one is secure from earthly power.

MARIA CELESTE: It will be so. It must. The father who conceived me, the Church which conceives us all, both serve a single master. The work to which I was sacrificed is my heart, whose nourishing currents sustain my soul, which belongs to God. Should the heart

fail, the soul must perish. God will save the soul, if our will is strong enough. You will help, Benedetto?
CASTELLI: I lack your enviable certainty.
MARIA CELESTE: Not my certainty. His. The certainty of his triumph. He is supported in the palm of God, and I in his.
CASTELLI: Should he choose silence. What of you?
MARIA CELESTE: This. (*She turns her hand over and places her palm in the candle flame. Castelli reaches forward and removes it.*)
CASTELLI: I will try, Maria. Within limits.
MARIA CELESTE: What limits?
CASTELLI: The limits of my small wisdom to comprehend his driven genius.
MARIA CELESTE: Outleap your limits, Castelli. He will lift you.

(*Galileo enters, embraces Maria Celeste and then Castelli. He drops into the couch in the manner of one who has just completed some great exertion. After a moment of silent rest, he leans forward, his head on his hands. Castelli and Maria Celeste have each taken a chair facing him.*)

MARIA CELESTE: Oh, Father, how wonderful it is to have you back with us. I prayed to God every night for your safe return. There is so much plague. (*Brightening, she reaches into a rough cloth bag.*) I brought you some preserves—your favorites, apricot and quince. I made them myself, late at night, after my duties were completed.

(*Galileo looks up during this little monologue, his expression becomes calmer, he leans forward and gently strokes her hair. She shudders at the touch.*)

CASTELLI: Your spirits seem strong. We were concerned.
GALILEO: Concerned. Why concerned? The trip was a triumph.

My work completely vindicated. Cardinal Bellarmine himself gave complete freedom to all my works and to the studies I intend.

CASTELLI: There have been rumors at court.

GALILEO (*displaying letter*): Which Bellarmine's personal testament will dissolve.

CASTELLI: We have also heard privately from Ciampoli.

GALILEO (*his forced ebullience disappearing*): So you know. (*pauses*) Ah, Benedetto, Benedetto, the governance of the world is in the hands of fools. (*laughs*) I must devise a telescope to see the truth beneath men's words, more darkly hidden than the stars of Jupiter.

CASTELLI: It could have been worse, Master. We might have been forbidden to discuss the Copernican assumption.

GALILEO: Assumption! Hypothesis! Convenience! We are allowed to play a game and must wear a mask when we play. And, as you say, truly, only fortune's whim permits that much. I was a fool to be tricked into a discussion of Scripture. It does not touch my business.

CASTELLI: You are not prohibited from discoveries.

GALILEO: Their proclamation to be returned only by mocking echoes from the empty Tuscan hills. Unbearable!

MARIA CELESTE: You are allowed to think. And the force of that thought will, one day, breach the gates of Rome.

GALILEO: The walls of Rome have no ears.

MARIA CELESTE: They can open to those who hear. You will help the Church, Father; and they will recognize your greatness. In serving you both, I will be allowed some tiny part in that great event.

GALILEO: Would I shared your faith.

MARIA CELESTE: You allowed me an education. Use it. Let me help your writings and warn against phrases that might delight your enemies.

GALILEO: It would be useful. Much time is wasted in transcription.

CASTELLI: And I will stay with you, Master, to study and keep uninvited visitors from consuming your hours.
GALILEO: Look! (*holding up papers*) In the coach from Rome, I sought formulas to explain the flight of an arrow after it leaves the bow. Aristotle says . . . (*pausing, reflectively, then continuing*) You see, I am most absurdly caged. I pray for silence, but the rebellious mind cannot be subdued. I would not think. But still I think. It is an illness death alone can heal. (*pauses*) There is a small villa in Arcetri. We will live there. It is a beautiful spot, and only a short distance from the convent.
CASTELLI: What shall we do now?
GALILEO: Do? Why, join the Grand Duke for dinner to celebrate my triumph. And then, to Arcetri.
CASTELLI: For how long?
GALILEO: Until the time for silence has passed. (*They follow him through a door to the throne room.*)

SCENE SIXTEEN

(*A single cone of overhead light illuminates a closely grouped assemblage of "pigeons"—delle Colombe, Magini, Caccini, Lorini, and, for the first time, Archbishop Mazzimedici.*)

MAZZIMEDICI: I could barely digest my meal. He was full of himself, more than ever . . . puffed up . . . belching anecdotes. (*sarcastically imitative*) How he overwhelmed some Aristotelian, delighted Prince Cesi's guests. How the Roman nobles waited patiently for a turn at his new spyglass. How amiably he conversed with Cardinal this and Archbishop that. And . . . oh yes, there was much reference to his new "friend," Cardinal Bellarmine. You would think him returned from a triumphal tour. The Grand Duke thought so. He couldn't hear enough. The man is more in favor than before. (*turning to Lorini*) And what about you, Father Lorini? You denounced him to the Inquisition.

LORINI: I didn't denounce him . . . not exactly . . . I mean, the stories weren't mine . . . I was told . . . I repeated them . . . only what I heard. Most of it from all of you. It was a matter of conscience. Only my duty. God knows I didn't judge the man.

DELLE COLOMBE: Let us be calm. We did what Catholic morality required. The decisions were made by others.

CACCINI: Are you so sure? Do you know how the men of Rome refer to Galileo's enemies in Florence? (*pausing*) We are called "pigeons," after you, Ludovici, your last name. Colombe. (*The others start to laugh. But delle Colombe is not amused. His sternness aborts the laughter.*)

MAGINI: If Galileo is to be king of philosophy, we had best map paths to refuge from his rule.

DELLE COLOMBE: The doctrines of Copernicus are condemned, and his most powerful disciple restored to Florence, untouched, his heretical pursuits unhindered, carrying tributes from the Holy Office. Incomprehensible! Seeking his condemnation, we achieved his vindication.

CACCINI: The reality is quite different.

MAZZIMEDICI: How do you know?

CACCINI: As assistant to the Commissary-General, I observed Galileo's meeting with Bellarmine.

MAZZIMEDICI (*in some surprise*): The Commissary-General?

CACCINI: Galileo escaped total disgrace by this only. (*He holds up a hand, thumb and forefinger outstretched and separated by a fraction of an inch.*)

DELLE COLOMBE: But how?

CACCINI: My lips are sealed. But fear not. He has powerful enemies in Rome; they await only the cause to overwhelm him utterly. The man has been allowed to discuss an idea, yet not believe it. A perilous line, easily crossed, even by accident.
MAGINI: He has already crossed. We all know he crossed. How could it have escaped the notice of Rome?
DELLE COLOMBE: Galileo has no taste for martyrdom. But he cannot stop himself. It is his nature. He thirsts for fame . . . unlike old Copernicus, he is not content to abide the judgment of posterity.
CACCINI: I may help speed the day. I have been assigned to Rome, as an assistant in the Congregation of the Holy Office.
MAZZIMEDICI: Felicitations, Caccini. At least one man has advanced himself in this affair. Most brilliant. Many advance by success; only the most subtle minds can wrest promotion from a failed cause.
DELLE COLOMBE: You said the time was not right. Will the time ever be right?
CACCINI: When things change.
DELLE COLOMBE: And when will that be?
CACCINI: When the time for change has come. It will come, my friend. It always comes.

SCENE SEVENTEEN

(The curtain is closed. It is August, in the year of our Lord 1623. From a small opening in the floor in front of the curtain, a thin column of white smoke begins to rise. There is silence. Then we hear the distant cheering of a crowd, which grows louder as the distance seems to diminish. As the noise crescendos, the curtain opens to reveal the bal-

cony of St. Peter's surrealistically suspended in space. Silence falls as an aged cardinal, fully robed, appears on the balcony and lifts his right hand.)

CARDINAL: Annuntio vobis gaudium magnum; habemus papem. [I announce to you a great joy; we have a pope.] (*There is a roar from the crowd, partially obscuring the next phrase, so that we are uncertain of the name.*) His Eminence the Most Reverend Lord Cardinal Barberini (*noise dying away so the rest is clearly heard*), who has chosen to be called Urban, the eighth of that name.

(*The cardinal stands silently and alone on the balcony; then steps to the back as Cardinal Barberini enters, dressed in a white silk cassock, purple mantle trimmed with ermine, and a gold-embroidered white stole. The tumult of the crowd continues as he raises his hand in benediction. From this perspective his naturally large figure seems to assume almost gigantic proportions.*)

SCENE EIGHTEEN

(*A few weeks later. Galileo's workshop in Arcetri. Present are Galileo, Salviatti, Sagredo, and Castelli.*)

SALVIATTI: Ambassador Niccolini reports that a visit would please the Pope.
CASTELLI: Now you can complete the dialogue.
SAGREDO: What dialogue?
GALILEO: A debate between the followers of Aristotle and Copernicus.
SAGREDO: Surely, you have written no such a work.

GALILEO: I could not bring myself to undertake the years of labor, knowing the unread manuscripts might be burned at my death.
CASTELLI: Finally, a Pope who understands the value of philosophy. The work must begin at once.
SALVIATTI: Not yet. Galileo's enemies remain in Rome. Popes are mortal. One cannot know where power will reside at the work's completion. You must insulate yourself from future hazards. Go to Rome, reveal your intentions, and secure his consent.
CASTELLI: Go quickly. The novelty of great power, when all seems possible, will kindle him to generosity.
SAGREDO: I am of an old and noble family, bred to the ways of power. Barberini is friendly. He has admired your work, spoken of you in the most flattering terms. But he is not what he was. He is Pope. The power of the Church has been entrusted to his care. You and your universe can have small weight in that balance.
GALILEO: My years are in descent; the chance may not return.
SAGREDO: Spend your years unraveling the mysteries of creation, not as missionary to an uncaring world. The truths you learn cannot be destroyed by an earthly power. Stay, Galileo, and let the stars alone! Let fools be fools. Why should you court martyrdom to win them from their folly?
GALILEO: I am a teacher, Sagredo, and have a duty of instruction. I cannot make disciples from the tomb. I must go.

(*Signora Marina Tedaldi, Galileo's mistress, enters, slightly breathless. In her mid-forties, the years have not destroyed a voluptuousness of body and manner. Her dress indicates that she comes from the upper echelons of society.*)

TEDALDI: Galileo! (*halting as she sees the others*)
GALILEO: Signora Tedaldi is a friend (*pauses*) of the family. (*to*

Tedaldi) We will be through in a few minutes, Marina, then I can join you in the garden.
TEDALDI: But, Galileo, it can't wait a moment. I ran almost all the way.

(*Sagredo, Salviatti, and Castelli start toward the door.*)

GALILEO: Please, stay. (*to Tedaldi*) These are my oldest friends, you can speak freely.
TEDALDI: Wonderful. Such nice friends. Don't you think my precious Galileo looks well? I wish he wouldn't work so much. Even the brain needs a rest. That's what I tell him. Isn't this true?
GALILEO (*gently*): There was something urgent.
TEDALDI: Have you heard? Our new Pope. But of course you have. I'm always the last to know. But this Pope . . . who is it . . . Clement?
CASTELLI: Urban, Urban the eighth.
TEDALDI: Why, he's Barberini. He's your friend, the man you told me so much about.
GALILEO: I did know him as Cardinal.
TEDALDI: Your friend! The Pope! Imagine! I know you will be going to see him, and you must ask one thing for me, just as soon as you can.
GALILEO: Ask? What?
TEDALDI: An indulgence. A plenary indulgence. My precious, there is plague everywhere. Two people on my street died of it this week. I am terrified. To be struck down suddenly, without time to do penance for all my sins, my soul sent to eternal damnation. Eternal! To burn forever! Perhaps even worse! And with only a word, the Holy Father—your friend—can grant me an indul-

gence . . . and my soul will ascend into Paradise at the hand of God.
GALILEO: I am not familiar with the procedure.
TEDALDI: It can be done. I know it can be done. My friend Andrea Portago. I've known her all my life. Just a few years ago, while she was sick, she talked to her brother. He's only a bishop. And in just a few weeks he brought her an indulgence straight from the Vatican. Her salvation was assured. Unfortunately she recovered. I don't think the indulgence covers things you do after it is granted. But that doesn't matter to me. After you bring it back, I will go to mass every day. But you must go right away. Your friend must want to see you. The plague. It can come as swiftly as a storm cloud on the ocean. So quick, and then it's over. You will do it, won't you, my darling Galileo? You must. Eternity is so very long . . . so very, very long. (*exits*)
GALILEO: Castelli, bring me the *occhialle*. (*to others*) It is something new I'm working on. It magnifies very small objects. I thought of bringing one to Rome, as a gift.

NOTE TO SCENE NINETEEN

The international conditions that confronted Pope Urban VIII when his reign began help to explain his motives in acting as he did, and, later, the intensity of his reaction to Galileo.

Like his predecessor, Urban VIII had two main goals: to restore the authority of the Roman Catholic Church within now heretic states, and to prevent Spanish power, allied with Emperor Ferdinand, from controlling Italy, including the Papal States. The Pope saw in France, and in Cardinal Richelieu, the only nation and leader that shared both these goals, but many powerful elements in the Church were convinced that only

Hapsburg power could restore the faith—and refused to believe that the imperial power was any threat to the territory of the Church or to the authority of the Pope. Among these groups, the Jesuits were the most important.

The significance of the Jesuits had increased with the advance of the Counter-Reformation, which they spearheaded. When Barberini became Pope, among the unfinished business of his predecessor he found decrees canonizing the founders of the Jesuit order—which he issued. Most of the Church's representation at the imperial court in Prague was in the hands of Jesuits. They were obedient, but, because it was necessary for Urban to maintain a great deal of ambiguity, they were unaware of any resistance by Rome to their identification of the Catholic cause with the fortunes of the Emperor. Naturally, a few were acute enough to know of the Pope's fears, but that same acuteness let them understand that the Pope could not afford openly to deny an identity between the Catholic and the imperial causes.

The Pope's intentions were, however, eventually disclosed—perhaps to a few intimates—but primarily through events. In 1624, the year this scene takes place, the Catholic League seemed on the way to victory, and the Pope's principal concern was to resist Spanish pretensions in Italy, which materialized when the imperial armies, goaded to action by Spain, attacked the Duchy of Mantua, virtually on the border of the Papal States. It was this action which alienated the Pope from the imperial cause, precipitated the final division of the Catholic cause, and led to the search for Protestant allies to redress the balance. (Urban said he was so worried about Spanish spies in the Vatican that he had trouble sleeping and had all the birds in the Vatican gardens killed lest their chirping disturb him.)

By the time of Galileo's trial, eight years later, the Holy Roman Empire had been smashed, and the Protestant armies of Sweden were virtually at the gate of Italy. It was uncertain whether France could control its Swedish allies, and any hope of ending the Protestant heresy in Europe was gone forever. Spain had been halted, but the Reformation was ratified, and there were new dangers to Italy. Urban's policy may then have seemed even more of a failure than it was to prove, for he ultimately did succeed in eliminating threats to the territory of the Church and to the rest of Italy. The frustration of Urban's ambition to reestablish the hegemony of the universal church—sensed if not yet grasped—had made most urgent the need to sustain the purity of an embattled faith. The misfortunes of war were to be mirrored in the misfortunes of Galileo.

There was another consequence of these events. Thirty years of unrestrained warfare, a butchery that reduced the population of Central Europe by at least one-third, also smashed the power of the lesser nobility in France, Spain, and parts of Germany. The result was a centralization of authority in what would later be called the nation-state, the distinctive political creation of the post-Renaissance world.

SCENE NINETEEN

(*The throne room of Pope Urban VIII, five or six months into the first year of his reign. Present are Francesco Cardinal Barberini, the Pope's nephew, a tall, well-fashioned man of twenty-six, made a cardinal in October 1623; Ciampoli; Father Grassi, who has risen to the highest ranks of the Jesuit order; Lorenzo Magalotti, brother of the Pope's sister-in-law, the Pope's Secretary of State, a bishop soon to be made a cardinal; and Lorenzo Bernini, a sculptor, who is standing to the side, working on a sketch of Urban.*)

URBAN (*angrily*): Urbino! Urbino is ours! Magalotti. You are Our Secretary of State. Inform the Emperor. It is an Italian dukedom under the rule of the Papal States.
MAGALOTTI: He does not deny your claim.
URBAN: Then why does he send German troops to Italy?

CIAMPOLI (*softly*): Francesco Niccolini, Ambassador from the Grand Duke of Tuscany, Your Holiness, in the company of Galileo Galilei.
URBAN: Have them wait.
MAGALOTTI: He complains that the presence of French troops in Urbino is intolerable to his Spanish cousin.
URBAN: Intolerable! The Spanish are intolerable! The French are there at Our request. We Ourselves asked them to protect Urbino. It is at Our northern frontier. Spain intervened without Our permission . . . against Our will . . . against Our sovereign rights. So, now they ask the Emperor to reinforce them . . . to fight Catholics. (*pausing*) Despite their boasted hordes and tubs of gold, they seem unable to expel a few French regiments, obstructed, no doubt, by the hand of God. Where is Chancellor Richelieu?
MAGALOTTI: He comes.
URBAN: They are greedy, that's all . . . greedy and idle. The Emperor's army is restless; he will now dispatch them from northernmost Europe to Italy, so they can add to their plunder. Magalotti! Go! Immediately! Instruct the Emperor that his troops are forbidden from our territories.
MAGALOTTI: I will, Your Holiness . . . once again. (*He leaves.*)
URBAN (*becoming calm*): We shall not allow this lawless quarrel to tarnish the glory of the time. From Sicily to the Baltic forts, all Europe is restored to Catholic rule. The savages of the New World are made Catholics. And yesterday . . . received just yesterday . . . the Emperor of Ethiopia submitted his ancient empire to the Roman Church. (*turning to Bernini*) You are fortunate, Bernini, that your time of creation coincides with Our reign. But we are twice blessed that Our reign is privileged to companion the lifetime of the immortal Lorenzo Bernini. (*Bernini silently acknowledges the Pope's flattery.*) Through your art, we shall place the stamp of Our restoring time on eternal Rome. (*to all*) We have already begun to construct a massive dome, finely decorated by scenes

of Our own choosing, to be set on twisted pillars, above the resting place of St. Peter. (*turning to Bernini*) How does work proceed, Lorenzo?

BERNINI: The plans are almost complete, Your Holiness, but Rome lacks bronze to fortify the dome.

URBAN: Surely there is bronze to be found.

FRANCESCO (*interceding*): Your Holiness, not long ago, in Greece, I viewed the pagan monuments.

URBAN: And?

FRANCESCO: Along the great arches of the Parthenon . . . enough bronze for four such domes.

URBAN: Strip the bronze from the Parthenon! You shall have what you need, Lorenzo. The rest will be melted for cannon to defend Castel Gandolfo. (*Francesco bows in acknowledgment and leaves.*) No one is dearer to our heart than Francesco Barberini, our first nephew and the first to be named a cardinal.

CIAMPOLI: Shall I admit Niccolini?

URBAN (*nodding, smiling*): And Galileo. (*Francesco whispers in his ear.*) Wait, Giovanni. (*He signals to the guard at the door.*) Admit Chancellor Richelieu. (*Richelieu enters, walks to the throne, kneels and kisses the papal ring, and resumes standing. Urban addresses the others present.*) Please leave us. Ciampoli and my nephew will remain. (*The rest exit, leaving the four men.*)

RICHELIEU: Your Holiness, if I may—

URBAN: What news from Urbino?

RICHELIEU: We can repel the Spanish. They are few in number, unaccustomed to the mountains.

URBAN: Good.

RICHELIEU: But the imperial armies would overwhelm our small garrisons.

URBAN: And rule Urbino.

RICHELIEU: In your name.

URBAN (*contemptuously*): In my name! The Emperor will ignore my commands and I lack means to compel him. (*pauses*) So, Chancellor, the danger you foretold now comes to Italy.

RICHELIEU: Perhaps not, Your Holiness. My ambassadors have met with the King of Sweden.

URBAN: Gustavus?

RICHELIEU: Gustavus Adolphus. A ruler fierce in combat and ambitious beyond his means.

URBAN: And very far away.

RICHELIEU: Exactly his advantage. And ours. Should he cross the Baltic and assault the German fortifications, Ferdinand will be unable to withdraw his defending troops to Italy.

URBAN: Is this Gustavus so foolish, to risk his own destruction?

RICHELIEU: Not foolish. A man, let us say, of excessive confidence. I am assured that if France supports him, he is prepared to sail. But without Rome's approval, I dare not confederate with a Protestant ruler lest I forfeit Catholic support for Louis's sovereign claims.

URBAN: Adolphus is Protestant.

RICHELIEU: Once danger has passed, we will have him withdraw . . . suitably rewarded.

URBAN: To spill Catholic blood with Protestant swords . . . we must consider this painful matter. (*Richelieu exits.*) Admit Ambassador Niccolini. (*The Captain of the Guards escorts Niccolini in. He approaches the throne, kneels and kisses the papal ring, and rises. Urban stands to embrace the Ambassador.*) It is always such a pleasure.

NICCOLINI: News of your ascension has been joyously received in every province of Tuscany.

URBAN: Convey Our gratitude. Inform the Grand Duke, no place shall be dearer to Our heart than the city of Our youth. As further sign of favor, tell him that Giovanni Ciampoli of Tuscany will be Our Master of the Briefs . . . Our strong right hand, now, as in all past years. So you see . . . a Tuscan Pope surrounded by men of Tuscany. You have brought me something to equal the return of Urbino—Galileo. Does he prosper? Bring him to us. (*He signals to the guard to admit Galileo, who enters, approaches the Pope, and kneels and kisses the papal ring.*) Welcome, Galileo. We are anxious to talk. Greet Our royal court. (*applause*) We expect Galileo to lead a new flourishing of philosophy. Have you new marvels to report?

GALILEO: I have many discoveries, Your Holiness. But they have not been published, for fear that enemies would distort my views. But the Almighty has allowed us a Pope who also is a philosopher.

URBAN (*flattered*): Not a philosopher, Galileo. But at least a man of Florence, one who understands that the light of philosophy can enhance the radiance of faith. As for what happened many years ago, had it been up to us, the matter would never have arisen. We cannot abolish the past. Still, it has left you free to discuss, and we intend to allow that freedom its furthest bound.

GALILEO: The affair has left a most unfortunate impression in other countries: that we Italians reject Copernicus not out of holy faith but because we do not understand him.

URBAN (*smiling*): Galileo not understand?

GALILEO: I would like to correct this impression.

URBAN: In what form?

GALILEO: I thought to present the evidence for our understanding in the form of a discussion between the followers of Copernicus and the supporters of Aristotle and Ptolemy, a dialogue which contains arguments of all schools, in language which every educated man will comprehend.

URBAN: You will preface this work by explaining its reason?

GALILEO: Of course.

URBAN: Good. We both have enemies. The times are turbulent. It is best to speak clearly so men cannot conjecture harm. Do you have a title?

GALILEO: *On the Flux and Reflux of the Tides.*

URBAN (*puzzled*): The tides?

GALILEO: The movement of water in the ocean basins as evidence of a moving earth. If one holds a pan of water, the

liquid is dormant; the fluid moves only when the pan itself is moved.
FRANCESCO: I have heard some claim the tides are captive to the moon.
GALILEO: A Protestant. Johannes Kepler. Does the moon have hands to stir the seas? A piece of mystic absurdity, alien to true philosophy.
URBAN: We do not think your title wise. The ignorant might suspect you provide physical proof for the motion of the earth. No one must have cause to contend that we impose necessity on the Lord.
GALILEO: I shall change the title, confining all reference to the tides within the text.
URBAN (*continuing*): You believe in the omnipotence of God?
GALILEO: Of course, Your Holiness.
URBAN: An omnipotent God could have given the world any form he wished, even one we cannot imagine?
GALILEO: That is so.
URBAN: He also created our senses, did He not?
GALILEO: Yes. So we might understand the glory of His Creation.
URBAN: Perhaps. He could also, if He so willed, have us perceive the world in any fashion—in conformity with His reality or, like Harlequin's mask, costumed to deceive the eye.
GALILEO: If He wished to conceal himself with a jest, He could. (*He says nothing to indicate disagreement, although this is basic to their conflict of understanding and conviction.*)
URBAN (*continuing to a triumphant, somewhat self-satisfied conclusion*): He may have willed that His reality match the appearance. I myself am much inclined to that opinion. But it is only an opinion. To assert He must have done so would deny His omnipotence. We see what we see or we see what He will have us see. The

subtleties of the Almighty are infinite, are they not, my dear Galileo?

GALILEO: They are, Your Holiness.

URBAN: That must be clearly expressed. (*pauses*) On this matter of a title. I have an idea. Since it is a dialogue, why not call it such —*A Dialogue on the Two Chief World Systems*.

GALILEO: A marvelous idea, Your Holiness. You will be proud of this work. My labors will evidence the ascension of faith under the glory of your reign.

URBAN: It is as we would have it.

GALILEO: If Your Holiness permits, I have brought a small gift. (*He reaches behind him to a table on which he has placed what appears to be a narrow tube about nine or ten inches long, held at a 30-degree angle from the table by a wooden stand.*)

URBAN (*Leaning forward curiously*): What is it?

GALILEO: I call it *occhialle*. The reverse of the spyglass, it magnifies small objects most wondrously. (*Urban reaches for the* occhialle, *which, as Galileo continues, he sets down carefully on an arm of the throne.*) I have examined with delight a great number of animals, among which the bug is the most horrible, the gnat and moth most beautiful. A fly appears the size of a lamb, covered with hair, and with sharp-pointed nails that enable it to walk feet upward.

URBAN (*starts to look into the* occhialle, *then looks up*): Francesco, bring me an animal . . . a moth, perhaps.

GALILEO: One is already fixed. (*He departs, his interview terminated.*)

URBAN (*peering delightedly into the* occhialle, *then turning to Ciampoli*): We have no choice.

CIAMPOLI: The Swede?

URBAN (*aside, to himself*): My other self. (*aloud*) Urbino cannot be allowed them.

CIAMPOLI: Shall we admit a barbarian Lutheran king to Catholic Germany?

URBAN: It is not we who have done this. They have done this. The Spanish and their German cousin. Shall an Emperor rule in Rome?

CIAMPOLI: Shall we risk return of heresy to Europe?

URBAN: There is no course without danger. Better confined to Baltic shores than invited to the gates of Italy.

CIAMPOLI: Can it be confined?

URBAN: Richelieu will be in control. (*pausing*) When I was a simple priest, Giovanni, I never doubted my salvation. As a cardinal, occasionally there were doubts. Now! Now I tremble daily for my immortal soul. But there is no help for it. Our Lord has entrusted us with the safety of His earthly church. That obligation is greater than any owed ourselves. Go to Richelieu. Tell him we must be cautious; our outward show impartial. But he will have our moral support for his Catholics. And our money for his Swedes. (*Ciampoli exits. Urban and Francesco remain.*) When Bellarmine was alive, he received an opinion from the Qualifiers of the Holy Office concerning this Copernican question. It raised the possibility of heresy. I do not believe it was ever published.

FRANCESCO: I have never heard of it, Your Holiness.

URBAN: Only an advisory opinion. It decides nothing, binds no one. One might place it among the archives of the Holy Office.

FRANCESCO: As a papal decree?

URBAN: No. We shall have nothing to do with it.

FRANCESCO: What cause, then—

URBAN (*interrupting*): Let it be printed. (*more softly*) Just a precaution, Francesco, just a precaution.

Note

In the course of their discussion, Urban has set forth four requirements. First, Galileo must explain that he is writing to prove that, if Italians reject Copernicus, it is out of faith and not because they do not understand the arguments. Second, the argument for Copernicus must be hypothetical, and well balanced by the arguments for Aristotle and Ptolemy. Third, the title of the book must contain no implication that there is an actual physical proof for the movement of the earth. Fourth, it must be clearly agreed by all disputants that God—being omnipotent—could have created the universe in an infinity of ways and could also cause it to appear to us in any way He wished, whether or not that appearance matched reality; thus, the matter must remain forever mysterious.

Galileo accepts these conditions. Indeed, he has no choice. He regards them as formal disclaimers necessary to permit publication of most of his dialogue. (There was a similar disclaimer in the preface to Copernicus' work.) The word "formalities" summarizes the differences between the two men. To Galileo, that is all they are. He will conform to them in a way that will not keep the intelligent reader from understanding that he is reading the most powerful argument for Copernican theory and for scientific method ever written. Pope Urban, however, does believe that the structure of the universe is an eternal mystery; that any theory must be truly hypothetical; that man has no right to assume that his powers of observation and reason impose limits on the Divine will.

ACT THREE

(*The curtain displays a cloak, whose lines hint that it covers the back of a huge human figure with head bent, leaving us uncertain if he is totally concealed or imaginary. The cloak is sulfur-colored and covered with painted flames and the figures of animated, laughing devils. It is the garb worn to the stake by a condemned man.*

(A tall, very slender man, completely clad in black, rushes, almost skipping, to the center of the stage. He looks at the audience, then—as if following their gaze—turns toward the curtain, then back, his hand in a sweeping gesture of display along his costume.)

I have nothing to do with burning people, I wear black because it is expected; the trademark of Scaramouche, the most famous actor in Italy. (*pausing*) Italians would know me in any color, but I often entertain in the less civilized provinces. I don't understand the coincidence, but it never fails: the lower the culture, the fatter the people, especially the men—not the young ones, but those of my own age. (*He turns to display his straight slimness.*)

See. A typical Italian. (*He looks back at the curtain.*) That . . . a man who wears that is a fool. Anyone who gets himself barbecued just hasn't learned that in Italy one can believe anything if he says the right thing or, even better, say anything if he knows how to make people think he doesn't mean it. Most Italians are good at that. And I'm the best. It's my trade . . . and I'm the king of my trade. (*He clears his throat, as if in preparation for something quite serious, and begins to recite.*)

> Philosophy, that leaned on heaven, before,
> Shrinks to her second cause and is no more.
> Physic of Metaphysic begs defense
> And Metaphysic calls for aid on sense!
> See mystery to Mathematics fly!
> In vain! They gaze, turn giddy, rave and die.

See!

(*He skips offstage.*)

SCENE ONE

(Galileo's workshop in Arcetri, several years later. On a small worktable are seen some scattered papers, a bottle of ink, and a large quill pen. Galileo, his back to the audience, paces back and forth in front of the table, then comes to a stop.)

GALILEO: So, my friends . . . Sagredo, Salviatti . . . the favored moment has come at last. What your death abolished, I will, in part, restore . . . your names, now launched on the immortal river of time, carried toward the sight of awaking centuries. Dearest Salviatti, let me wear your face, and use your tongue to relate discoveries of mine, and of farseeing Copernicus. *(As he speaks the light on him fades and rises on Salviatti, standing across the worktable.)* Next the Ptolemy, the Aristotle, of this mortal masquerade. *(The actor who played delle Colombe in earlier scenes appears.)* I shall lend you the name of Simplicio, whose ancient commentaries on Aristotle burden our shelves. But how to be evenhanded in this business . . . to moderate our discourse with skeptic interrogation . . . I lack the temperament . . . Let me grant it, Sagredo, to you, whose judicious caution far exceeds my own. *(During this, light rises to illuminate Sagredo. Still in profile, Galileo picks up his pen and speaks to the three men before him as the last remaining light still on him is extinguished.)* What an invention! The greatest in the story of our world: this writing. By a few simple symbols . . . to send one's thoughts over vast intervals of space . . . across time . . . to let the dead speak. Speak, now, Sagredo, to those who will hear you a millennium hence. *(As he finishes, Galileo is in darkness. There is the vague suggestion of a palace where Sagredo is welcoming the others. There are murmured civilities.)*

SALVIATTI: Truly, Simplicio, can you not understand that Aristotle assumes what is really in question? It is an abuse of logic.
SIMPLICIO (DELLE COLOMBE): Please, Salviatti. It is he who invented the very forms of logic.
SALVIATTI: Should I allow you to expose my errors, you must permit me to question yours . . . or those of your master . . . if we are to investigate the merits of these world systems.
SIMPLICIO: And what value, to replace his philosophy with yours?
SAGREDO: The truth is its own value.
SALVIATTI: So it is, but it bears other fruit.
SIMPLICIO: Of what kind?
SALVIATTI: To understand Creation is to command the energies of Creation . . . (*Lights dim as his thoughts trail off.*)

SCENE TWO

(*Galileo has taken a seat, with his back to the audience, at the same small table. Now the entire workshop is visible. In front of the desk, a few feet away and perpendicular to it, stands another, longer table whose surface has been carefully polished, in contrast to the rugged wood of the other furniture. This is where Galileo conducts experiments. On it and elsewhere around the room are some of his creations—a telescope, a thermoscope, the military compass, and a large lodestone whose magnetic power has been increased by being sheathed in metal. On the desk is a golden astrolabe, modeling the cosmic spheres in accordance with the traditional conception.*

(*Galileo is writing. A large manuscript is neatly piled in front of him. He stops writing, lays his pen aside, and sits back in his chair, staring at the single sheet in his right hand. The Tuscan hills, visible through the windows, reflect the reddening light of dawn. Maria Celeste enters from behind.*

ACT THREE

(Hearing her come, Galileo wheels abruptly to face the audience. Seven or eight years have passed. He is a changed man: visibly aged, hair and beard gray, face lined with the wear of incessant toil—but still possessed of his full faculties and native vigor.)

MARIA CELESTE (*solicitously disapproving*): Father, still awake?
GALILEO (*interrupting*): It is finished, Maria.
MARIA CELESTE: Finished?
GALILEO (*leaning back, and reading with mounting exuberance*): Sì. Listen. *Dialogue of Galileo Galilei—Chief Mathematician at the University of Pisa and First Philosopher and Mathematician to the Most Serene Grand Duke of Tuscany—In which is set forth four days of discussion concerning the Two Chief World Systems, Ptolemaic and Copernican—Propounding Equally the Arguments on Each Side!* (*pauses*) How does that sound?
MARIA CELESTE: Eight years of labor. (*She starts toward Galileo as if to embrace him, then stops.*) We must thank the Almighty for strengthening you to this fulfillment. (*She stands in silent prayer for a moment and then crosses herself. Galileo crosses himself at the same time.*)
GALILEO: And you also, Maria, who have freed me from the cares of daily life.
MARIA CELESTE: You would have finished, Father, had you been abandoned to a mountaintop. I almost trembled to witness such devotion.
GALILEO: Trembled?
MARIA CELESTE: For our souls, Father. But these were the fears of an ignorant woman. Perhaps because I felt such pleasure at serving you. But now it must end. (*Galileo looks at Maria as she talks, his attention for the first time wholly concentrated on his daughter, his expression loving but shadowed with doubt.*)
GALILEO: Maria, when I sent you to the convent you were so very

young. A woman . . . one as beautiful as you have become might have found a more abundant life.

MARIA CELESTE: I found comfort in prayer before the picture on my wall.

GALILEO: I looked much younger then.

MARIA CELESTE: Not the eyes. They burn now as they burned then. But you should leave for the world of the illustrious which awaits you.

GALILEO: I shall soon return. This work will draw world enough to Arcetri. And I have more to do. Now I must apply to the clerks of the Church for the holy imprimatur.

MARIA CELESTE: It cannot be denied.

GALILEO: I have carefully observed the precautions urged upon me by the Holy Father. Even the title is his. Still, meticulous obedience will not be my sole reliance. Many years ago, I learned—most eloquently instructed—that my qualifications were better adapted to follow the paths of planets than the corridors of Rome. There is no justification for refusal. But there are ways to retard and postpone approval, until the supplicant is safely tucked beneath his earthen blanket.

MARIA CELESTE: The Pope himself is friendly to your cause.

GALILEO: Popes have no friends. But this Pope has a mind. And he did encourage me. There are others, less sympathetic, who may try to keep the matter from his decision. But I also have friends of influence and worldly skills. They will see us swiftly through. (*pauses*) Has Castelli arrived?

(*Maria goes to the door, opens it, and returns with Castelli.*)

GALILEO (*handing him the manuscript*): Package it firmly, Benedetto. I will take it to Rome for the license.

CASTELLI: It is unnecessary.

GALILEO: Unnecessary? I cannot circulate a work without a formal license. It is the law of the Church.
CASTELLI: Not the license. The trip. The Papal States have been strictly quarantined against the plague, excluding all not bound on urgent matters of state.
GALILEO: Must I await the pleasure of the plague?
CASTELLI: It is all arranged. Ciampoli will review the manuscript to confirm compliance with the instructions of the Holy Father. For detailed scrutiny and revision, you will consult the Inquisitor of Florence, specially delegated by Rome.
GALILEO: Can he grant the imprimatur?
CASTELLI: You will have two. One from Rome, another from Florence.
GALILEO: Our Inquisitor is very pious, and very old, and very ignorant.
CASTELLI: So much the better. (*He exits with the manuscript.*)
GALILEO: And now, Maria, you and I, the saint and the philosopher, together we lean on the hinge of the world.

SCENE THREE

(*The court of Grand Duke Cosimo. Present are the Grand Duke and Duchess, Castelli, Galileo, Maria Celeste, Niccolini, and Andrea Cigoli.*)

GRAND DUKE (*to Galileo*): Ambassador Niccolini has arrived from Rome carrying many requests for your book. It seems there are no copies in Rome, not one.
NICCOLINI: A cause of annoyance. The book has circulated for almost five months.

GALILEO: Every road to the Papal States was sealed to quarantine the southward flow of plague.
CASTELLI: The problem, my lord, as I understand it, was not the paper or the ink but anxiety over the animal hides used to bind the pages.
GALILEO: It no longer matters. Copies have arrived in the bookstalls of Rome, my dear Niccolini, since your departure.
NICCOLINI: I hope one remains.
GALILEO: Take this. (*He hands him a large leather-bound work.*) Inscribed with my gratitude.

(*The Grand Duke rises and leaves, accompanied by the Grand Duchess. The others bow deferentially, and then follow him out, leaving Galileo alone with Niccolini. Together, they enter the adjoining private anteroom.*)

NICCOLINI (*his tone subdued, but triumphant, tapping the book*): So. It is accomplished. The star of Tuscany shines once more.
GALILEO: With your help, Francesco.
NICCOLINI: And many others. (*begins to smile, perhaps chuckle*) Animal hides! (*again caresses the cover of the book*) Whose thought was that? How ingenious! (*Galileo starts to say something, but Niccolini continues.*) It no longer matters. Now the book has its own life.
GALILEO: Without you, it might have been stillborn.
NICCOLINI: The gratitude is mine, for being allowed to assist, even slightly, a moment of rare creation.
GALILEO: I hope it pleases you.
NICCOLINI: I fear your text will exceed my slight knowledge of philosophy and mathematics.
GALILEO: I wrote it for you.
NICCOLINI (*laughs*): For me? Friends need no flattery.
GALILEO: For men like you—educated in the old learning, curious

about the new. I write in the Italian of the streets, bringing philosophy to those who will direct our future.

NICCOLINI: If you have done that . . . (*pausing*) But I am anxious to begin.

(*Galileo leaves. A servant comes in to extinguish the lights. Niccolini motions him to leave the light which illuminates his chair and the pages of the book. The servant leaves Niccolini sitting in the darkened room, reading. Gradually the solitary light dims until Niccolini is in darkness. Behind him, on what appears to be an empty expanse of stage or, perhaps, a raised circular platform, a cone of light reveals three men standing; were they all diagrammed, they would be each at the corner of an equilateral triangle. They are Sagredo, Salviatti, and Simplicio. Having shown the familiar trio, the light dims and the curtain falls.*)

SCENE FOUR

(*Stage left, at the front, before the closed curtain, is a large tent of neutral, drab color, its flap open to a substantial interior. It is the tent of Gustavus Adolphus, King of Sweden and active commander of the Swedish army. Inside, sitting on a wooden camp chair, is a tall, thin man, costumed and plumed as if in attendance at the French court, a dress that appears pretentious, even foppish, in these surroundings. He is an emissary from Chancellor Richelieu. Standing outside the tent, and to its left, concealed from the Frenchman's view, is a man wearing black pants, boots, and jacket, an Englishman of medium stature, his features ruggedly austere, almost peaked.*

(*Two men enter stage left, moving toward the tent. Both are dressed in the disheveled, drab uniform of ordinary Swedish soldiers and are distinguished only by their swords, sheathed at their sides. The first,*

Gustavus Adolphus, is short, with a large, almost oversized head set on a thick, muscular frame. His luxuriant, tousled hair and beard are flaming red. Behind him walks General Oxenstierna, his second-in-command, a fairly tall man but without the King's bulk. His hair, less luxuriant, is matted and very blond.)

ADOLPHUS: The name? This place? Here . . . where we will fight?
OXENSTIERNA: Lützen.
ADOLPHUS: The battle of Lützen it shall be! After this victory, Austria alone will divide us from the Alpine passes. (*He claps his companion on the shoulder.*) A long way from Sweden, Oxenstierna. (*He notices the man in black, halts, and confronts him.*) What species is this?
ENGLISHMAN: From England. You must be Gustavus Adolphus, King of Sweden?
ADOLPHUS: And of much more by now. Do you come to watch the spectacle, or to study the art of victory? A citizens' army. That's the secret. They will beat mercenaries every time.
ENGLISHMAN: The King of England compliments your success and tenders England's gratitude that you have liberated Northern Europe from Popish rule.
ADOLPHUS: Indeed I have. Pushed Lutheran princes back upon their thrones almost before they struck the ground. But your king. He is no Lutheran.
ENGLISHMAN: We left Rome a century ago.
ADOLPHUS: Divorced Rome. To bed a queen. The Church of England—nothing but Catholics without the Pope. The English will worship anything that does not obstruct their lust.
ENGLISHMAN: What shall I tell the King?
ADOLPHUS: That Northern Europe has been cleansed of his enemies, his Catholic enemies. Further, that I intend a thorough scrubbing for the entire continent. (*He turns, begins to move toward his tent, stops, and, half turning back, speaks over his shoulder.*) Tell

him I'd like to visit England, with my companions. He needn't worry about the Channel. We build good boats in Sweden. (*He enters the tent, sees the Frenchman.*) What, another one! General Oxenstierna, is this a battlefield or an opera house?

(*The Frenchman rises, looks puzzled, and a little frightened. He is unable to identify the Swedes. Adolphus strides across the tent, picks up a large cape of finely woven bright red wool, trimmed in ermine, and drapes it about him.*)

FRENCHMAN: You are the King? (*He drops to his knees.*)
OXENSTIERNA: He comes from Richelieu.
ADOLPHUS: Get up.
FRENCHMAN: I did not recognize . . . your clothes.
ADOLPHUS: Fighting clothes. Get up.
FRENCHMAN: You do not wear your cape?
ADOLPHUS: And make myself a target for every lunatic German in search of passage to Valhalla? For God's sake, man, get up. Get up, I said. Get up!
FRENCHMAN (*rising*): You ride into battle like a common soldier?
ADOLPHUS: Common! I am a king. I came to fight. What good is a king in a box?
FRENCHMAN: Safer.
OXENSTIERNA: They fight harder in his sight.
ADOLPHUS: Battle is to begin. Your business . . . quickly. Did you bring my money?
FRENCHMAN: It is coming.
ADOLPHUS: Coming! I need it now. My men expect to be paid. They fight better that way. And certain items, food, for example, and powder, are most useful for wars. They cost money.
FRENCHMAN: Surely, it must have been sent.
ADOLPHUS: Surely! . . . Must have! . . . Sent! Arrive, man! I am only interested in Arrive! Must I march to Paris myself? Richelieu

is obliged. We have an agreement, which I must enforce, if he will not honor it. (*He pauses, dismissively.*) Well, the gold is not in your packs. We have work to do.

FRENCHMAN: The Chancellor sends—

ADOLPHUS: Words! He sends words, when my need is gold.

FRENCHMAN: Word that all France admires your victories over the imperial army.

ADOLPHUS: Victories, man? We shattered them. Slaughtered and scattered and swept them from the field—German, Spanish, it made no difference, fractured by the fist of Sweden. And they have not escaped yet.

FRENCHMAN: That was the substance of the Chancellor's message. He is pleased you have accomplished what you agreed, and more. Urbino is restored. Neither France nor Italy need fear the imperial armies. Their power is broken beyond restoration.

ADOLPHUS: Do not omit the Lutheran princes, whose fear I have also purged. Their thrones, their lands, and their faith—which is my faith also—are forever secured from swinish Catholic gluttony.

FRENCHMAN: Precisely. Chancellor Richelieu wishes you what you deserve . . . high honors, wealth, and a place in the rule of Europe . . . to take in triumph back to Sweden.

ADOLPHUS: To Sweden? I'm not going back to Sweden. Not now. (*He points outside the tent.*) Look man, out there, there's almost half of Europe I haven't seen.

FRENCHMAN: He . . . the Chancellor . . . says you have reached the limits of agreement and must stop.

ADOLPHUS: Stop? Why stop, when it is just as easy to go forward? Who can stop me? Can Richelieu stop me? Tell him, tell your Lord Chancellor, your Cardinal, should he send twenty thousand Frenchmen against me, I will take them (*reaching out and grabbing the Frenchman by the hair, who, astonished, shrinks back but does not break the King's painful grip*) like this, and return him twenty thousand corpses to impregnate the soil of France. (*He releases the*

Frenchman and lowers his voice.) Tell him to send the money. (*He throws off his cloak.*) There is war to be made.

(*Adolphus and Oxenstierna leave. The French envoy sits down. Long moments pass. There is the sound of hoofbeats and shouts from a rider.*)

—Victory! The Spanish are running! Another victory!

(*The Frenchman puts his head in his hands, despondent. After a few silent moments, four Swedish soldiers enter bearing a litter which carries the body of Gustavus Adolphus. Oxenstierna follows. One of the soldiers speaks to the man beside him.*)

—It was an accident. A stray ball from . . . no one knows. The battle was already won.
FRENCHMAN (*rising*): Your king is dead?
OXENSTIERNA: He knew the risk.
FRENCHMAN: You command the army?
OXENSTIERNA: A body without a heart. I must bring him to Stockholm, to the Queen. We shall reconsider.
FRENCHMAN: The Protestant princes will tremble.
OXENSTIERNA: Perhaps, but not tumble. The Catholic strength is gone. We have seen to that.

(*The lights dim.*)

SCENE FIVE

(*A light rises on Niccolini, still reading. Behind him, in a narrow cone of light, stand the trio of the* Dialogue.)

SALVIATTI: At least we have agreed on this: Our frail faculties are all subject to the correction of omnipotent God.

SAGREDO: Let this be the conclusion of our four days' argument. Now, according to our custom, let us go and enjoy an hour of refreshment in the gondola that awaits us.

(*The cone of light snaps off. The trio is gone. The lamp beside Niccolini's chair slowly brightens. At the same time, the night darkness at the window is displaced by the pale red of dawn. Niccolini turns the last page, closes the book softly, leans over and snuffs out the light. Slowly, thoughtfully, he puts the book down on an adjacent table, rises, steps toward the window, and stands silently looking out, as the sun rises over the green Tuscan hills.*)

NICCOLINI: And who, until now, has known what this Copernican question was all about? (*He looks down, stamps his foot as if to test the firmness of the floor, his voice beginning to rise as his excitement grows.*) It moves! I move! We are all in motion, all of us, tumbling through the heavens! And, after this (*looks toward book*), we will never come to rest again. (*He pauses.*) Ever since the ascension of Our Lord, we have thought ourselves condemned to this earthly platform, eternally fixed in struggle, held, unaided, midway between Divine salvation and the chambers of the damned. Poor, lowly animals, bound to the surface of corruption . . . immobile, amid whirling celestial spheres. And now (*his voice rises, his excitement now manifest, and he almost begins to laugh*) we move! Like God's great stars to travel the heavens, where there is neither above nor below, here nor there, only that which was and that which is to be. And how is this mighty liberation accomplished? Not through antique texts. By *these hands* . . . *these eyes* . . . *this brain*. The skull of a single man imprisons the power to unravel Creation, to compass and describe the entire world . . . Why . . . if this is so . . . we may regain the dominion granted Adam in our days of innocence. Creatures who can accomplish this, with such powers . . . they are almost like . . . gods. (*Suddenly he is silent, and looks around him. There is no stirring. It is early. Niccolini starts to leave, pauses, looks toward the sun, now above the horizon.*) My Galileo, my friend, may God watch over you.

(*He exits into the throne room.*)

SCENE SIX

(*The lights go up on the throne room, in which the same group present in Scene Three has assembled, with the addition of a formally dressed official who is whispering to the Grand Duke. It is the messenger from Prague. Cosimo listens attentively, then, looking very pleased, rises, strides over to Galileo, embraces him wordlessly, then turns to the others.*)

GRAND DUKE: It is beyond all expectations. (*He motions to the messenger.*)
MESSENGER (*glancing at documents*): Fulgencio Micanzio of Vienna has said it is the greatest work of the age. From Paris, Thomas Campanella writes that all learning is now prostrate at the feet of great Galileo.
COSIMO (*impatiently takes papers from the messenger, holds them aloft*): And more, much more. Princes, scholars, my own cousin Marie de' Medici writes from Paris. More for you, Galileo, than I ever had from the bitch. Here is one from a man called Harvey. I am told he is the greatest doctor in England.
NICCOLINI: And from Rome?
CIGOLI (*who has not joined in the general exuberance*): Nothing yet, my lord.

MARIA CELESTE (*to Galileo*): His Holiness will be greatly pleased. For He personally encouraged you in this labor.
CASTELLI: And fortune has contrived that your work enters Rome, not a solitary supplicant, but in triumph, heralded by the cheers of all Europe.
GALILEO: Yes, fortune . . . with a little help, my dear Benedetto.

SCENE SEVEN

(*The stage is dark. At the side is a door over which is a sign: "B. Landini—Printer." One man, closely followed by two others, approaches the door. All three are cloaked and cowled in the familiar, darkly ominous attire of the Dominican order. Although the features of all three men are obscured, and will remain so throughout the scene, their leader is the aged Inquisitor-General of Florence, Giacinto Stefani, who had licensed the manuscript for printing. He approaches the door and knocks with a surprising firmness for an old man. He is holding a parchment scroll, unrolled far enough to expose a large red seal.*)

LANDINI (*from inside*): I'm coming. For God's sake, man, I'm coming. (*The Inquisitor-General knocks again.*) Patience. Softly. You think this the gate to heaven? (*He opens the door. He is a man in his forties, wearing a printer's ink-stained apron and radiating unmistakable and cheery vitality. He looks surprised, but not stunned or especially fearful. He bows his head in a gesture of respect.*) Sorry, Father. I thought it one of the young poets from the university.
INQUISITOR (*interrupting, in formal tones*): Signor Landini?
LANDINI (*arrested by the tone*): Yes, Reverend Father?
INQUISITOR: Printer of the works of Galileo?
LANDINI: I have been so honored.

INQUISITOR (*reading from the parchment in the tone of official proclamation*): As Inquisitor-General of the City of Florence, I have been commanded by the Sacred Congregation of the Holy Office to halt all publication of the works of Signor Galileo Galilei and to confiscate all remaining copies of his work.
LANDINI (*swiftly recovering from surprise*): There are no books, Father.
INQUISITOR (*the official tone breaking*): No books?
LANDINI: They were sold as quickly as I could print them.
INQUISITOR: Nevertheless, this order binds you. (*He hands him the parchment.*)

(*The trio starts to turn away.*)

LANDINI: What of Galileo?
INQUISITOR: The Holy Office has summoned him to Rome.
LANDINI: The Inquisition! But he is very old, and has been sick.
INQUISITOR: He will go by choice, or in chains.

(*The Dominican officials leave.*)

LANDINI (*to himself*): The Grand Duke will never allow it. I'll save the type. This fuss will make the book more valuable.

(*He closes the door. He can be heard humming to himself as he walks through his shop.*)

SCENE EIGHT

(*The court of Grand Duke Cosimo. Present are the Grand Duke, Galileo, Maria Celeste, Niccolini, Andrea Cigoli, Castelli, Archbishop*

Mazzimedici, and Federigo Morosini. This last is the senior member of the most distinguished patrician family in Venice, formerly a magistrate of the Venetian Republic and now a revered elder statesman, whose house Galileo had frequently visited during his tenure at Pisa. Galileo, seated, seems absorbed, almost oblivious to the surrounding discourse.)

COSIMO (*to Cigoli*): Inconceivable, Andrea! An outrage! In my city! To my Chief Philosopher! Without discussion! You are my Secretary of State. Inform them of our indignation. (*pauses*) No. Our annoyance.
CIGOLI: It is not customary for the Holy Office to notify secular authorities.
COSIMO: Customary! It is not a question of custom. It is not customary for us to have our sovereignty ignored. It is not customary for the Church to license a work and then to forbid it! It is not customary to allow a man the homage of Europe and then summon him like some lunatic prophet of the streets.
CIGOLI: There may be some irregularities—
COSIMO: That *is* a custom, a Roman custom. The custom of confusion. The same confusion which has brought the devil Swede to the gates of Italy. And, should they enter, who will greet them? Tuscany! And, of course (*gesturing toward Morosini*) our Venetian friends, who have sent the noble Signor Morosini to concert measures of protection. (*He pauses.*) Indeed, Signor Morosini, I believe you know Galileo.
MOROSINI: We met frequently when he taught in Venice.
CIGOLI: Defiance of the Holy Office would heap further dangers on perils already grave. The matter must be carefully considered.
MOROSINI: When the Inquisition commanded a philosopher at Venice, we refused the summons.
CIGOLI: You do not have papal armies on your border.
COSIMO: Father Castelli, what is your opinion? The meaning of

this summons? You are often in Rome, adviser to the Vatican itself.

CASTELLI: On matters of hydraulic engineering.

COSIMO: You are consulted on waterworks, but your ears are not deaf to other topics.

CASTELLI: There are as many stories as voices, my lord. It is no secret that Galileo has enemies in Rome. The hostility of the "pigeons" has been hardened by failure. Many Jesuits are offended by Galileo's exposure of their philosophers. Undoubtedly, the most envious of these have conspired to persuade the Holy Office that the *Dialogue* may contain some transgression of faith, or even personal offense directed at the Holy Father.

GALILEO: A pretense! A preposterous pretense. Their true grievance is the sight of their windy scholarship scattered by the force of reason.

CASTELLI: In Rome every whispered falsehood can find an idle ear.

COSIMO (*to Galileo*): Perhaps you should visit Rome. Not because of this unlawful summons. To dissolve these jealous distortions directly. Obviously the matter has not been considered, not by men of rank. In Rome, you will be barricaded by noble friends of high position. The Holy Father himself has praised you to us. And I will send you—if you decide to go—cloaked in the full dignity and love of the Grand Duke of Tuscany. What do you think, Galileo?

GALILEO (*softly*): As Your Excellency wishes . . .

COSIMO: Your protection is my only wish. And to expunge this malicious blemish. (*He pauses and turns to Niccolini.*) Niccolini, what is your opinion?

NICCOLINI: Much the same as Castelli, my lord. Some conspiracy has gained the ear of the Holy Office.

COSIMO: Have you communicated with Ciampoli? Giovanni would know the reason of this reversal.

NICCOLINI: I have sent messages, but without reply.

Cosimo: No one spends August in Rome. Not by choice. Ciampoli must be at the ocean. He will return before Galileo arrives.
Niccolini: In Rome I heard nothing particular, no describable cause of alarm . . . Yet still, I seemed to detect . . . no sign I can name . . . a sense of expectant menace, formless, unspoken. Officials of the Sacred Congregation made unusual calls on the Embassy of no disclosed purpose except to inquire after Your Serene Highness and Galileo. Such unprecedented interest, from such quarters, was troubling. I think it best if Galileo remain with us until present angers abate.
Cigoli: You suggest we should defy the Holy Office?
Niccolini: Failure to resist may imperil Galileo.
Cigoli: Eagerness to resist will imperil Tuscany.
Cosimo (*admonishingly, to Cigoli*): We will not let fear resolve this issue. Archbishop, you are learned in the laws of Rome.
Mazzimedici: I have never attended proceedings of the Holy Office. However, under the law, Galileo's position is impregnable.
Cosimo (*somewhat eagerly*): How impregnable?
Mazzimedici: He submitted his work for examination and received the imprimatur. He cannot be prosecuted for publishing a work which the Church formally approved.
Cigoli: I agree. The summons mentions neither prosecution nor trial. It is merely an invitation to the Holy Office.
Castelli: Invitation! An order!
Cigoli: An order, then. But not to appear for trial.
Cosimo: Perhaps we have exaggerated the gravity of this matter. Yet can we rely on the license, a flimsy seal?
Mazzimedici: The Holy Office would never transgress its own constitution. And even without the license, Galileo could not be examined for heresy. The Copernican doctrine has never been declared a heresy.
Cosimo: So our Galileo is doubly protected—by the license and by the absence of heresy.

NICCOLINI: The law is a treacherous shield from those who make the laws.
MAZZIMEDICI: The Church can change its laws but not ignore them.
NICCOLINI: The Pope's power is absolute.
MAZZIMEDICI: Precisely why Rome so meticulously observes procedures. Authority so terrible is secure only if it checks itself. Of all sovereigns, Rome is the most legalistic.
COSIMO: And Urban is Galileo's friend.
CASTELLI: It is too great a risk.

(*Galileo stands abruptly, interrupting the discussion, aroused as if from lethargy, which may only have reflected intense concentration. His voice is forceful.*)

GALILEO: I will go to Rome. Of course I will go to Rome. I have committed no transgression. My *Dialogue* was permitted by the Pope himself. All his precautions have been observed. A refusal to go would be read as fear, fear as failure of conviction, failure as falsehood. I would be seen as the living denial of all I have lived for, and believe.
NICCOLINI: You would go to vindicate your work?
GALILEO: In hope of vindication. But even without hope, I would go. I have no taste for punishment, but I would not violate the laws of the Church. For sixty years I have been a believing and obedient Catholic. I will die so. (*He pauses, looks around the room, begins to smile.*) Not so grave, my friends. It is easy to slander from a distance. I do not intend to destroy my enemies. I will heal them, uncurtain their blindness with the sweet light of reason. I go by order. I shall return by will.
CASTELLI: Master, are you sure? Is Rome grown more congenial since you last—
GALILEO (*almost roaring*): Last time! Last time I was forced to

debate with fools, around dinner tables, my demonstrations conducted to the clamor of rumbling bellies and sodden jests. (*more quietly, but still with force*) This time, my dear Benedetto, this time, I will address the cardinals of the Holy Office and answer to them directly.

MOROSINI: Will you risk your person to save your philosophy?

GALILEO (*looking at Morosini, almost startled, as if he had not previously noted his presence*): Ah, Federigo. How good to see you, my old friend. What wonderful days, at your house in Venice—our young heads spinning with your old wine and my new ideas, the stars staring silver-eyed from black canals, so close it seemed we could touch the heavens. No, Federigo. Quite the contrary. I go to submit my person to the destiny of my philosophy. The argument is not about the passage of the sun and earth, even less is its object, Galileo. The Holy Church, the chosen instrument of Our Lord, must pursue the revelations of natural philosophy, whose force can be ridden, but not resisted.

CASTELLI: Your enemies understand the ways of Rome better than you.

GALILEO: True. But those of highest rank are ambitious only for the Holy Church. Their obligation to advance the faith will forbid denial of the truth. I must go.

GRAND DUKE (*enormously relieved*): You shall be carried in my personal litter. Everything will be paid for. (*He rises and leaves, accompanied by Cigoli and Niccolini.*)

GALILEO (*turning toward Maria Celeste and embracing her*): And you, my darling.

MARIA CELESTE: My lord.

GALILEO: Your counsel?

MARIA CELESTE: God does not permit His chosen servants to war between themselves.

COSIMO: You do not fear for your father?

MARIA CELESTE: I fear only his refusal.
GALILEO: It would go easier if your health permitted me your company. While I am gone you must not neglect your infirmities.
MARIA CELESTE: The chills will soon pass. We are used to them. I will continue my peculiar part: to recommend you to Our Lord God continually, which is also my duty, not only as your daughter but as a desolate orphan which I should be if you were taken from me. For after God, I belong to you, excepting only that I would not offend His Divine Majesty.

(*Galileo releases his daughter and begins to leave. Morosini approaches him. They are the last people left in the room, except for the Archbishop, who is in a far corner talking to an attendant.*)

MOROSINI (*speaking softly*): I have been empowered by the Senate to offer you the asylum of Venice. The arm of Rome will not reach you there. You can continue your studies and write as you please. Time will vindicate your works.
GALILEO: I am grateful, but I cannot. I am too old to wait amid unread manuscripts until the world is willing to look at itself. I will soon be dead, Federigo. This chance may not come to me again—to try, with waning strength, gates which have been locked for centuries.
MOROSINI: Will your science of motion assist you?
GALILEO: No, but it will be justified.
MOROSINI: A Delphic phrase?
GALILEO: The headsman's ax and the coronation crown descend according to the same law. (*There is a momentary silence.*) I have often thought of Sagredo's counsel. "Stay in Venice," he said, "you will enjoy greater security from the laws of a republic than from the whims of a monarch."

MOROSINI: The choice was yours. You thought Florence the more glorious. Now you make another journey. To your glory, Galileo. (*He lifts his hand in a kind of salute. They leave, as does the attendant who had been talking with the Archbishop.*)

(*The light narrows in on Mazzimedici, alone in the empty room, speaking to himself.*)

MAZZIMEDICI: I have performed my part. The rest belongs to Rome.

SCENE NINE

(*We are in the spacious offices of Francesco Cardinal Barberini, who, as "Cardinal-Nephew," is the Secretary ex officio of the Holy Office. The room is decorated with works of art. On various stands, one sees a Galilean telescope, an* occhialle, *and the older astrolabe. The Cardinal, physically almost a young version of his uncle, is sitting at his desk. Facing him is Father Vincenzo Maculano, known as Firenzuola, after his place of origin. Firenzuola is Commissary-General of the Inquisition—that is, he is responsible for conducting Inquisition proceedings, subject to the supervision and review of a committee of cardinals assigned to the Sacred Congregation of the Holy Office. On this committee, the Cardinal-Nephew is first among equals. To use an American metaphor, Firenzuola's position is analogous to that of the Chairman of the Joint Chiefs of Staff; the cardinals occupy the office of the Secretary of Defense; the Pope is Commander in Chief and Head of State.*

(*Firenzuola does not fit the stereotype we are likely to imagine when we hear the label "Inquisitor." He is a tall, lean man whose gentle appearance and honesty of manner are no deception. He is himself something of a scientist. Seven years from now, he will be somewhat surprised when Urban VIII makes him a cardinal, and reflect that the Pope's action might have something to do with that old, half-forgotten case of Galileo: perhaps because he was useful, or because he was used, although his silence was due not to discretion or personal loyalty but to obedience to the requirement of secrecy imposed on all participants in the proceedings of the Holy Office.*

(Firenzuola feels no prosecutorial zeal toward an accused man, takes no satisfaction in the torture, threats, and terror sometimes required to break a man's will, finds no fulfillment in the sight of a helpless and broken defendant at the mercy of his court, feels neither vengeful nor righteous when imposing often terrible penalties. In fact, as a man he finds much of this distasteful. But he has a job to perform, a high obligation in service to the Church and to the Catholic faith. Christ Himself gave the Church spiritual authority on earth so it might guide mankind in the ways of salvation. Heresy was a challenge, a danger to that authority, and must be destroyed for the sake of man's immortal soul. This is not only his mandate but his faith.

(This case is specially troublesome. He knows that Galileo's immense reputation is founded on real achievements. Although the man has been contentious in matters of philosophy, he has always been a faithful and obedient Catholic. His transgressions did not challenge the central dogmas of salvation, as did those of Bruno or Luther or Calvin. At best, they concern matters of marginal importance—scientific doctrines that were discussed by Copernicus a century ago and that the Church had never formally condemned. If the man had offended, he must be condemned, but it could be done gently. Galileo was one of the glories of the Catholic world. He was very old, beset by illness, and would soon be summoned before a far wiser judge than the Inquisition of the Holy Office.)

FIRENZUOLA (*deferentially but firmly*): The law is clear. We can suppress a book that has been licensed, but we cannot prosecute the writer.
FRANCESCO: The learned but very old Inquisitor of Florence didn't understand a word of that book.
FIRENZUOLA: His authority was given by the Holy Father. The Church cannot make others pay for its mistakes.

(*An attendant opens the door and Ambassador Niccolini enters. Cardinal Francesco rises, greets Niccolini, smiling with a familiar embrace. Niccolini appears quite perturbed.*)

FRANCESCO: My dear Ambassador. How is the great man?
NICCOLINI (*stiffly*): Signor Galileo has arrived in Rome and is prepared to submit himself to the Holy Office in accordance with the customary procedure.
FRANCESCO: Customary procedure! Customary procedure has no place here. Do you think we would throw Europe's greatest philosopher into a dungeon? Is he here?
NICCOLINI: At the Embassy.
FRANCESCO: There he shall stay. Naturally, once proceedings have begun, some confinement is required. A nuisance, but necessary to protect the secrecy of the Inquisition.
NICCOLINI: Confined? Here? (*gesturing toward the stone Vatican buildings visible through the window*)
FRANCESCO: Not in prison. Of course not in prison. An apartment, most spacious, reserved for distinguished visitors. He may bring his own servant for the preparation of meals.
NICCOLINI: I am much relieved, Your Eminence, I had feared—
FRANCESCO: Shall we inflict Roman cooks on a Tuscan digestion?

Are we thought so cruel? He will be treated as befits his honored rank. Is that not so, Father?

(*Firenzuola, looking a little uncomfortable, nods agreement.*)

NICCOLINI: Will there be a trial?
FRANCESCO: Do not be too concerned. There will be formal procedures. Once a process like this is initiated, it can only be terminated in proper order, according to regulations. Had it been my decision, it would never have begun.
NICCOLINI: Who, then . . . ?
FRANCESCO (*interrupting*): Tell me. Your illustrious philosopher. It is rumored he is already embarked on a new work.
NICCOLINI: You have heard truly. The first pages of his new science—the science of motion—were completed before this interruption.
FRANCESCO: At his age, and in bad health . . . a whole new science! (*reflectively, partly to himself*) The years cannot restrain the mind of Galileo. It ascends past all infirmities. Much like my uncle. Age only increases the urgency of their pursuits, as if dwindling mortality compelled them irresistibly toward some completion.
FIRENZUOLA: Toward a restoration of faith.
FRANCESCO (*looking quizzically at Firenzuola*): Knowledge without faith transforms men into beasts, but faith without knowledge—that, Firenzuola, is very difficult to maintain. (*then, abruptly*) A dilemma. But not for us to resolve.

(*The door to the Cardinal's office opens. Ciampoli's familiar face is seen. He seems surprised to see the three men, and begins to close the door.*)

FRANCESCO (*calling out*): Giovanni, come in.
CIAMPOLI (*entering*): I thought you were alone. I came to say farewell.
FRANCESCO: It is no interruption. You know the Ambassador.
NICCOLINI: Farewell? Are you on a trip?
CIAMPOLI: I go to San Moreto.
FRANCESCO: Giovanni returns to more pastoral responsibilities.
NICCOLINI: But San Moreto? So remote a place.
CIAMPOLI (*smiling*): A lovely village, where one can escape attention from the great.
NICCOLINI: Galileo is here. He will be most anxious to see you.
CIAMPOLI: There is no time. I leave tonight. (*He takes leave of Firenzuola and the Cardinal, then embraces Niccolini closely, whispering.*) I am banished. Tell the great one to be cautious. The force behind the dart is very strong.

(*Ciampoli leaves, followed by Niccolini.*)

FIRENZUOLA (*deferentially but firmly*): The question of the license is difficult.
FRANCESCO: The Inquisitor merely ratified the views urged by Galileo's Tuscan followers . . . the Ambassador . . . (*pausing*) . . . and Ciampoli.
FIRENZUOLA: Persuasion is not unlawful . . . not without fraud.
FRANCESCO: Ah yes, fraud. And fraud as legally conceived can be deceitful act or willful failure to disclose important facts, is it not so? (*Firenzuola nods in agreement. He rises to go and moves toward the door.*) It would be well to remember, Father, that once the barriers to jurisdiction are navigated our problem is not whether to act, but how.

(*Firenzuola exits. Cardinal Barberini sits silently at his desk for a second or two, looking at documents. There is a knock at his door, and an assistant enters. He looks up.*)

FRANCESCO: They are here?
ASSISTANT: As you commanded.
FRANCESCO: Bring them in.

(*Father Caccini and Ludovici delle Colombe enter. The Cardinal somewhat abruptly motions them to seats. Although his manner is businesslike, even friendly, he cannot completely conceal an underlying contempt.*)

FRANCESCO: You know Galileo has been summoned by the Inquisition of the Holy Office?
DELLE COLOMBE (*almost too eagerly*): We do, Your Eminence.
CACCINI (*quietly cautious*): We have heard as much, Your Eminence.
FRANCESCO: And the reason?
DELLE COLOMBE: Concerning his latest work, the *Dialogue?*
CACCINI: Just rumors, Your Eminence, we have heard only rumors.
FRANCESCO: You are not friends to Galileo?
CACCINI: Not enemies.
DELLE COLOMBE: No personal grievance, none at all.
FRANCESCO: Was it you, Father Caccini, who denounced him fifteen years ago?
CACCINI: Others denounced him. I merely supported their testimony. Not from ill will. It seemed my obligation.
FRANCESCO: Such pious zeal has brought you a long way.
CACCINI (*electing not to notice the sardonic overtones*): Thank you, Your Eminence.

FRANCESCO: And you, delle Colombe? You were leader of the anti-Galileo faction in Florence?
DELLE COLOMBE: I am only a professor. Not a leader. I disagreed with his philosophy.
FRANCESCO: You were first to suspect the man a danger to the faith.
CACCINI: He was not condemned.
FRANCESCO: Your insight was not shared. It adds to your credit. He came most cleverly disguised.
DELLE COLOMBE: He has unmasked himself.
FRANCESCO: Not completely. True, the meaning of his book is obvious.
CACCINI: And cause for punishment?
FRANCESCO: Only if the meaning was intended by the author.
CACCINI: Which his caution has disclaimed, in the body of the work.
FRANCESCO: You have a nimble mind. We have the meaning, and we have the meaning's disavowal, implanting doubts—legal doubts—which make proof difficult.
CACCINI: Ordinarily, such doubts are resolved through interrogation.
FRANCESCO: Only if there is a prosecution.
DELLE COLOMBE: No trial!
FRANCESCO: The Inquisition lacks jurisdiction to try a writer whose work has been licensed.
CACCINI: Without jurisdiction, no trial. Without a trial, no interrogation.
FRANCESCO: I am relieved. You confirm my reading. Unless, of course, there was some fraud involved—if, for example, the writer failed to disclose some important facts.
DELLE COLOMBE (*excitedly*): Everyone knows the old Inquisitor was tricked. He understands nothing of philosophy. (*He immediately*

pulls back, aware that his impulsive words were imprudent, if not impious.)
FRANCESCO (*ignoring delle Colombe and smiling warmly at Caccini*): You were present when the works of Copernicus were suspended?
CACCINI: Yes, Your Eminence.
FRANCESCO: You were very young to be admitted to the proceedings?
CACCINI (*with a hint of braggadocio*): I was involved in everything.
FRANCESCO: How fortunate. The years have taken all the others. (*He continues as a smiling Caccini seems about to speak.*) We have heard of an injunction which forbade Galileo not only to defend the Copernican views but to discuss those views.
CACCINI: That is true, Your Eminence. I still have the injunction. However . . .
FRANCESCO (*again not letting Caccini continue*): Galileo did not mention an injunction when he requested the license. Failure to disclose the command of the Church would be fraud, if, of course, the injunction had been issued.
CACCINI: And this would invalidate the license?
FRANCESCO (*turning from Caccini to delle Colombe, affecting his most gracious and amiable manner*): Signor delle Colombe. Your mission here in Rome is scholarly?
DELLE COLOMBE: It is, Your Eminence.
FRANCESCO: To help your studies, you have been given access to the archives of the Holy Office. A rare privilege.
DELLE COLOMBE: Thank you, Your Eminence. My permission is limited to the subjects of my work.
FRANCESCO: You are guarded while you search these documents?
DELLE COLOMBE (*somewhat indignantly*): That would not be necessary.
FRANCESCO: Interesting. (*turning*) Father Caccini.
CACCINI: Yes, Your Eminence.

FRANCESCO: You have an opportunity to be of immense service. Memories so distant fade and disarrange themselves. But try. Recall as best you can whether the injunction was actually issued. Signor delle Colombe may be able to help you.
CACCINI: Help?
FRANCESCO: If your memory confirms an injunction, it should be noted in the Inquisition files. It would be unusual to omit some reference. Is that not so?
CACCINI: Unheard of. Men have accused the Inquisition of most varied and ingenious sins. No one has ever thought to condemn their paperwork.
FRANCESCO: We must all be equally meticulous. If you can help us observe all the forms of law, you need fear no response save gratitude. (*They look at each other. There is a knock at the door.*) I must attend an audience. (*They all start to rise.*) Please, finish your discussion here, in comfort. (*He leaves.*)
DELLE COLOMBE (*excitedly*): It has been accomplished.
CACCINI: Not by us.
DELLE COLOMBE: Naturally the Jesuits helped, and Mazzimedici.
CACCINI: Do you realize what we are to do?
DELLE COLOMBE: Of course. It will be simple. We are . . .
CACCINI: The force of the entire Jesuit order, combined with that of all Dominicans, could never commission such a deed.
DELLE COLOMBE: Who, then?
CACCINI: Somewhere so towered, even to guess would involve us in perils greater than those of Galileo. Let us go.

(*They rise and exit.*)

ACT THREE 171

SCENE TEN

(*A few weeks later. We are in Cardinal Barberini's office. He is at his desk, writing, when the Commissary-General knocks lightly and gently opens the door. Francesco motions for his visitor to enter.*)

FRANCESCO: The license no longer prevents a trial.
FIRENZUOLA: It is invalidated by Galileo's failure to disclose the injunction forbidding him to discuss the Copernican question.
FRANCESCO: Still, failure to obtain a valid license is not heresy.
FIRENZUOLA: Rejection of the Copernican doctrine has never been proclaimed an article of faith. It cannot be heresy to discuss it.
FRANCESCO: There is another form of heresy, is there not? Heresy *ex parte dicentis*, when the sinner deliberately opposes his will to that of the Church?
FIRENZUOLA: Rarely proven. We would have to demonstrate that Galileo himself believes in the Copernican doctrine and wrote to persuade others of its truth.
FRANCESCO: Exactly. That's exactly what he did.
FIRENZUOLA: He has observed all the formalities. The preface instructs that the discussion is only hypothetical. And he concludes, as the Holy Father requested, with agreement that a universe constructed by Transcendent Omnipotence could not be compassed by our poor understanding. (*beginning to smile*) He adds that he wishes the world to know that we Italians disavowed Copernicus out of faith, not because we could not understand him.
FRANCESCO: He certainly accomplished that. No one will ever have cause to doubt the Italian imagination. (*voice rising*) The book is heresy, the man heretic, his *Dialogue* the most powerful argument for Copernicus ever written. And everyone knows it. Shall we have men laugh that the Holy Office cannot read?
FIRENZUOLA: Shall we have men tremble that the Holy See rejects the rule of sacred law? Our interpretation is not proof. We must

demonstrate that Galileo himself, from defiance or excess of arrogance, deliberately wrote what he knew to be a defense of the Copernican doctrine.
FRANCESCO: What suffices as proof?
FIRENZUOLA: His own admission.
FRANCESCO: Then obtain it.
FIRENZUOLA: We are forbidden rigorous methods of interrogation for men of his advanced age.
FRANCESCO: To torture the old man into submission would convince no one. He must confess it himself.
FIRENZUOLA: He is reported to remain righteous in his own defense, convinced he behaved as an obedient son of the Church.
FRANCESCO: He does not know we have discovered the injunction?
FIRENZUOLA: I think not.
FRANCESCO: Everything is prepared?
FIRENZUOLA: Yes, Your Eminence. Galileo has been ordered to present himself tomorrow. He will be confined to the apartment you assigned him until his case is concluded.
FRANCESCO: Good. All Europe has notice of this proceeding; they must have no cause to complain of our treatment. (*pauses*) Let him wait a little, enough time to sense his true condition, shut off from the world, his fate in the hands of irresistible power. Then he will learn of the injunction. Once that blow has fallen, inform him that his admission of deceitful intent will ensure lenient treatment.
FIRENZUOLA: Would such a pledge be honored?
FRANCESCO: Do you doubt it?
FIRENZUOLA: We only recommend a sentence. Final decision is in the hands of others.
FRANCESCO: Then leave it to others.
FIRENZUOLA: It is my duty to conduct the trial. I am not obligated to persecute the man, or deceive him into guilt with promises that will not be kept.
FRANCESCO: You are obligated to serve the Church. (*more softly*)

We must not seem weak or irresolute in our support of the faith, lest we strengthen our foes. Certainly not in this matter, which is notorious throughout Europe.

FIRENZUOLA: I do not believe it will strengthen the faith for the Commissary-General to dishonor pledges made in the name of the Sacred Congregation.

FRANCESCO (*sternly*): That is not for you. Proceed. (*tone softens*) The Inquisition will not dishonor its pledges. All will happen in dutiful submission to authority.

FIRENZUOLA: I will try. But I am not hopeful. Galileo will never admit to wrongdoing, not while any hope remains.

CARDINAL: That is not within your power. Yet hope is already gone, and he will know it before you meet.

(*They both cross themselves, and the Commissary-General leaves.*)

SCENE ELEVEN

(*The papal throne room. Pope Urban VIII, despite his sixty-five years, has grown more formidable in the decade since his elevation, his frame amplified, his vitality undiminished, more confident, at ease, almost casual. A whitened beard and mustache give him a biblical appearance. Urban looks straight ahead as, to the side, Bernini sketches on a slim wooden easel. While he poses, the door opens, admitting the smiling Cardinal-Nephew accompanied by a somber Niccolini. Francesco motions Niccolini to halt, and turns toward the throne. The Pope, seemingly absorbed, has not looked at them.*)

FRANCESCO: Your Holiness. The Ambassador of His Most Serene Highness the Grand Duke of Tuscany.

(*Urban now smiles warmly and extends his hand, as Niccolini advances to kiss the papal ring. The Pope makes a brief gesture of benediction and motions Niccolini to be seated on a chairlike cushion which—in conformity to custom—rests a foot beneath the platform on which the Pope sits. The Cardinal-Nephew moves to the side and remains standing. He is to be an onlooker at this meeting.*)

NICCOLINI: I trust the Holy Father enjoyed his rest at Castel Gandolfo.
URBAN: You are kind, Ambassador, but the dangers of the time allow no rest. We remove ourselves from Rome's tumult to deliberate the meaning of events. (*He holds up his hand to Niccolini, indicating a halt in the conversation, and turns toward Bernini.*) Lorenzo. Surely you have all you need for the moment.
BERNINI: One more session. (*He begins to fold up his easel, takes his pad, prepares to leave.*)
NICCOLINI: I did not think Rome had room for another monument.
URBAN: This monument is of Ourselves. To adorn the chapel of St. Peter.
NICCOLINI: A monument to a living Pope? Is it permitted?
URBAN: Not until now. We permit it. (*pausing, the hint of megalomania dissipated by a smile*) Bernini may not outlive me. (*Bernini leaves.*)
NICCOLINI: The Grand Duke has asked me to convey his respects, and to request—
URBAN (*reflectively, as if not hearing Niccolini*): Not Our troubles only. We gave thought also to the dangers of Tuscany.
NICCOLINI (*warily*): Dangers, Your Holiness?
URBAN (*shifts to face Niccolini more directly, his tone, still gentle, becoming more businesslike*): There are rumors of secret agreements between Tuscany and Spain.

NICCOLINI: Spanish forces camp a day's march from our northern border. We must accommodate ourselves—
URBAN: Accommodate? Why? For protection? Against whom? The Swedes?
NICCOLINI: Adolphus is killed. His armies withdraw.
URBAN: Not due to your Spanish protectors. He died, struck by chance, while mocking their terrified flight from his conquering swords. You, like We Ourselves, can thank only the Lord of vengeance, who rendered retribution to the proud and shook from the neck of the Catholics their most bitter enemy. (*Urban crosses himself, as does Niccolini.*) The Spanish have no further purpose in Italy. No Catholic purpose. I wish them gone.
NICCOLINI: Still, Your Holiness, they are there.
URBAN: Grievously wounded by defeat, enfeebled by hunger and plague. There are other armies, to your south, unscarred, well armed, idle. My armies. Defenders of the Papal States. (*His voice rises in anger.*) Must all our subjects defy us? Last week Cardinal Borgia of Spain accused Us, before the entire consistory, to our face, of betraying the Catholic cause. Hypocrite! Intriguing, insolent, usurping hypocrite! It is Spain, his Spain, that set Catholic against Catholic in Urbino. It is Spain that would make the Catholic world, Our world, into a Spanish province. It is Spain, mercenary, ravenous Spain, that sought to obstruct Our goal, the single purpose of our reign, and forced us to unleash the Protestant sword. We had no choice. He left us no choice. The risk was forced upon us. Borgia knows this. His master knows this. The future chronicles of our time will confirm it. The man should be burned! But we can do nothing. (*pausing*) For the moment. We are not so helpless in Tuscany.
NICCOLINI: I will convey your views.
URBAN: Please do. (*Both men fall silent.*)
NICCOLINI: There is the question of Galileo.

URBAN: It is sent to the Holy Office.
NICCOLINI: He is Tuscany's most honored subject.
URBAN: He has discussed matters when his duty required silence.
NICCOLINI: The Grand Duke petitions Your Holiness intervene to protect—
URBAN (*rising, interrupting, in an outburst of passion*): Intervene! We are asked to intervene! We have already intervened! To halt the greatest scandal in the history of Christendom. Your Galileo has published his heresy to the world.
NICCOLINI (*surprised and taken aback by the Pope's anger*): His book bears the imprimatur of the Church.
URBAN: Inscribed by a withered, obsequious, simpleminded priest of Tuscany.
NICCOLINI: With your authority . . .
URBAN: Who was deceived into granting the license.
NICCOLINI: Deceived? How deceived?
URBAN: By Galileo. And by Ciampoli, Our Master of Briefs, the most intimate to Our will, who had the audacity to assure Us that Galileo wrote exactly as We had commanded . . .
NICCOLINI (*softly, almost to himself*): Ciampoli. Has this uncomprehended flame singed even Ciampoli?
URBAN: Your Galileo, your most honored subject, deliberately defied an injunction of the Holy Office, imposed many years ago, forbidding him to discuss the Copernican question.
NICCOLINI: I heard no mention of an injunction.
URBAN: Nor did anyone, although the order, its command unmistakable, has been discovered among the files of the Holy Office. Galileo concealed it when we discussed his plans. He concealed it from the Inquisitor of Florence who reviewed his book. He concealed it from Rome when he was published. It was a document of great relevance. It was his duty to disclose it, a duty of canon law, whose breach was fraud. Fraud obtained the license. The discovery of fraud erases the license.

NICCOLINI: To forget an old injunction, even conceal it, is not heresy.

URBAN: His book is heresy. His opinions are heresy.

NICCOLINI: It seems to me he holds the opinion that God, being omnipotent, could as easily make the world go round as not.

URBAN: Seems to you! Has every man in Tuscany become a theologian? Are you asking us, sir, to examine your views?

NICCOLINI: No, Your Holiness. I trespass on matters I do not understand.

URBAN: Withdraw from them. And advise the Grand Duke to do the same.

NICCOLINI: Signor Galileo does not wish favored treatment—

URBAN: We have given him favored treatment. Instead of a dungeon, he occupies rooms reserved to visitors of distinction. It is a favor which We personally commanded, the like of which has never before been granted.

NICCOLINI: He wants only a fair hearing, to answer his accusers and argue his case.

URBAN: That is not the custom of the Holy Office.

NICCOLINI: I do not understand.

URBAN (*his voice rising again*): It is not the custom, sir! Not the custom! The Holy Office does not give reasons to sinners. Its function, its only function, is to pronounce judgment and advise Us of the appropriate penalty.

NICCOLINI: There will be no trial?

URBAN: Trial! This is not a game for children. The man has offended the faith. He has only to confess his intentions and receive sentence.

NICCOLINI: Galileo intended no offense. All men are fallible. No man is more strict in Catholic obedience.

URBAN: Are we to play the fool, wear a demented's mask, pretend ignorance of what we know! What everyone knows! What he has told them! The man believes the earth circles the sun. And he knows what he believes. He has written a book to expound this doctrine. And he knows what he has written. He has tried to persuade others of its truth. And he knows what he intended.

NICCOLINI: He avowed no such purpose. The opposite—

URBAN (*interrupting*): The Inquisition has means to extract true intentions.

NICCOLINI (*somewhat helplessly*): But he is Chief Philosopher to the Grand Duke.

URBAN: Should His Serene Highness meddle in this business, he will not come out of it with honor.

NICCOLINI (*pleadingly*): Cannot this man be helped?

URBAN (*continuing angrily as if not hearing Niccolini*): It is a perverse business, a new doctrine, altogether contrary to Holy Scripture. May God also pardon Ciampoli. For he was a friend of this new philosophy and has a weakness for novel doctrine. (*pausing*) Help him? Did you say, "Help him"? I have already used him better than he used me. He betrayed his word. He made a joke of Christianity. He deceived Us!

NICCOLINI: This will destroy him.

URBAN: He has destroyed himself. For he knew what he was doing. (*His voice softens.*) But do not mistake us. We would not deal harshly with the man. The heresy must be condemned. But Galileo's person . . . he need not suffer greatly.

NICCOLINI: To whose hands does the penalty belong?

URBAN: Partly his own. You are his friend. He will be agitated, confused. He needs counsel, a reminder that the Inquisition deals more leniently with those who admit to transgression and repent. Intransigent heretics have often received most terrible penalties.

NICCOLINI: Surely, Holy Father, you cannot mean the dungeon or the stake? Not for Galileo.

URBAN: We have said nothing of the kind. It is not Our custom to threaten. Or to promise. We shall make Our decision when the matter is brought before us.

ACT THREE

(*Niccolini sits silently, shocked and in despair.*)

URBAN: Come, my dear Niccolini. (*Niccolini looks up at this sudden tone of gentle familiarity.*) It is not so grave. Most probably your Galileo will soon again be busy with his instruments and numbers. You are a wise man. You can help him. He is in need of wisdom.
NICCOLINI: Thank you, Your Holiness.
URBAN: You may visit with him if you wish. The guard will take you.

(*Niccolini rises to leave, moves toward the door.*)

URBAN: Should his accommodations be unsatisfactory in any way, inform Our nephew. He will remedy it.

(*Niccolini exits.*)

URBAN (*in a tired voice*): Great power brings great burdens. (*He looks toward his nephew.*) You do not understand, Francesco, do you?
FRANCESCO: Not entirely, Your Holiness.
URBAN: Niccolini does not understand. Galileo himself, the greatest mind in Christendom . . . he will not understand. It is good that it should be so difficult. Were it simple, few could resist the temptation which is offered. (*musingly*) But some will know. You have seized all the copies you could find?
FRANCESCO: Yes, Your Holiness.
URBAN: The frontiers have been closed to the passage of the book?
FRANCESCO: Most stringent measures have been taken.
URBAN (*relapsing into a musing tone*): But ideas have wings, Francesco. Can your guards pound in the crows? (*pausing*) You will want to talk with the Commissary-General. Our task has been accomplished.

FRANCESCO: Ciampoli is waiting.
URBAN: Here?
FRANCESCO: Just outside. I saw him as I entered.
URBAN (*sighs deeply*): My treasured Giovanni . . . why? (*He catches himself and, through a visible effort of will, reunites himself to his office.*) Instruct him to appear before Us.
FRANCESCO: It is only a book.
URBAN (*indicating Bible, softly*): Yes, only a book. (*Francesco bows deferentially, begins to leave, reaching the door when Urban's voice arrests him.*) The final decree of the Holy Office. Do not bring it for my signature. It is customary but not required. And, Francesco, it is not necessary that all ten cardinals be agreed. A simple majority is required. Do not sign.
FRANCESCO: But how can I avoid—
URBAN (*interrupting, in tone of command*): No name from the house of Barberini is to appear.

(*Francesco leaves. Ciampoli enters and approaches the Pope, kneels and kisses the papal ring, and stands.*)

URBAN: You leave for San Moreto?
CIAMPOLI: Tonight, Your Holiness.
URBAN: The roads are treacherous. Morning would be better.
CIAMPOLI: The command was most imperative.
URBAN: Morning will be soon enough.
CIAMPOLI: As Your Holiness wishes.
URBAN: It is a quiet place, San Moreto. You will have leisure for poetry.
CIAMPOLI: Truly. But, for me, an amateur's pleasure. I lack the gift.
URBAN: The founding premise of our Academy.
CIAMPOLI: Academy, Your Holiness?

CIAMPOLI: All you did was to serve Him and that only. Does that not comfort the pain of these bitter bafflements?
URBAN: There is no comfort in failure. (*pausing*) Even you, Giovanni, are taken from me.
CIAMPOLI: And Galileo . . . executed?
URBAN: Shall I enhance his fame, announce his blasphemy to an ignorant and distracted Europe? Once he recants and his works are banned, he will be placed under house arrest for the remainder of his life.
CIAMPOLI: He will not recant.
URBAN: Of course he will. He is an obedient Catholic. It is most important, for him, to be *thought* an obedient Catholic.
CIAMPOLI: By denying his life work?
URBAN: His works, thanks to you, Giovanni—in part, to you—can be found in every capital. We will burn what we can, forbid more to be printed. But there are many presses, and many printers. Even Galileo cannot cancel the lines he penned. No denial will diminish the seduction of his ideas. Why should he die for what is already accomplished?
CIAMPOLI: Seductive? How seductive?
URBAN: It allows all men to believe themselves masters of Creation.
CIAMPOLI: Equal to—
URBAN: God. (*pausing, then more formally*) I have no choice. Your crime was not one of intent. It was, however, an act damaging to the Church. As your friend, I understand. I forgive.
CIAMPOLI: But still I must be exiled?
URBAN: I have no choice. I am Pope . . . That is Our decision. (*Ciampoli turns and begins to leave, but his departure is arrested by Urban's voice.*) It is, you understand, a double exile. For me, too, there remain only the friendless years, alone, a passage walled by unloving, cold contention, reaching to the moment of extinction. (*Ciampoli has stood, unmoving, but without turning back, during these*

last remarks of Urban. He now resumes his exit. As he goes through the door, which has been opened by the guard, the Pope continues.) Think of me, Giovanni, in San Moreto . . . and in the innocence of your prayers.

SCENE TWELVE

(We are in the large drawing room of a spacious, artistically furnished apartment with a small adjoining chapel located on the upper floor of a Vatican building assigned to the Holy Office. Its large windows, overlooking St. Peter's Square, reveal the approach of dusk. On the wall is a tapestry of Canossa—the same scene as depicted in the painting we saw earlier in Cardinal Barberini's house. The door to the room opens on darkened Vatican corridors. Niccolini, having related his audience with the Pope, is departing, silent, his face grim. Galileo sits at a table with some scattered pages of manuscript, letters, and a pen, its tip still fresh with ink. He sits upright, his arms resting on the chair, absorbed so fixedly he appears almost paralyzed. In a moment, Father Firenzuola enters, but Galileo does not notice his entrance or his presence.)

FIRENZUOLA (*softly*): I am Father Firenzuola.
GALILEO (*momentarily startled, quickly calming himself*): I am your accused, Galileo Galilei, citizen of Florence.
FIRENZUOLA: I accuse no one. It is not my place. I am obliged to proceed against those accused by the Sacred Congregation of the Holy Office.
GALILEO: Ambassador Niccolini has told me everything. I am in your hands.
FIRENZUOLA: This occasion, for our first meeting. It is most un-

lucky. I have admired you from afar. No mind in Italy has greater reach.
GALILEO: You have an interest in natural philosophy?
FIRENZUOLA: Its modern progress excites my mind—often, unfortunately, beyond my comprehension. I am unable to complete Copernicus.
GALILEO: You have read his work?
FIRENZUOLA: Tried. A man of immense learning, but without your gift for exposition.
GALILEO: A fortunate deficiency. It preserved him from . . . this.
FIRENZUOLA: You remember Professor Libri, of Padua?
GALILEO: He refused to look through my spyglass, arguing that my discoveries were an illusion of the lens.
FIRENZUOLA: He died last Sunday. Perhaps if Libri did not see your celestial trifles while on earth, he will now that he has gone to heaven.

(*Galileo smiles broadly, then stands and, smile fading, walks to the window.*)

GALILEO: Look here, Father. (*Firenzuola joins Galileo at the window.*) The most miraculous moment of the day. Only the topmost fringe of the setting sun remains above the horizon. Yet it is enough to make all Rome blush pale rose. There (*points*), the evening star, whose brilliance the withdrawing sun can no longer hide. In a few moments, as the rim of day departs, it will be joined by an innumerable host to bespangle the roof of the world.
FIRENZUOLA: It is most beautiful.
GALILEO (*turning toward him*): Would I had never seen it! Would I had never gazed toward the heavens, that, like some penitent, I had fixed my eyes to the earth I walked upon!
FIRENZUOLA: You discovered many extraordinary things.
GALILEO: I discovered (*pausing, turns and points*) you!

FIRENZUOLA: This is not pleasant for me.
GALILEO: I believe you, Father. You are the instrument of a larger purpose. I once thought the same of myself. If I could now return, I would have made a grave for my instruments and all my studies. Instead, I dug one for myself.
FIRENZUOLA: You are made excessive by distress.
GALILEO: Should you send me to the stake, would that make the earth revolve around the sun if it does not now, or stop if it does?
FIRENZUOLA: You will find no grave in Rome.
GALILEO: I am already condemned. (*He returns to the table and sits.*)
FIRENZUOLA (*carefully*): Certain acts of yours must be condemned. But there is great latitude in choosing the penalty.
GALILEO: Can that choice be influenced?
FIRENZUOLA: Not directly. The Holy Office is most lenient toward an accused who evinces his repentance by helping them satisfy their obligations.
GALILEO: It does not seem you need my help.
FIRENZUOLA: You do not wholly understand the Inquisition. Our purpose is not punishment alone, but to reconcile the accused with the Catholic faith.
GALILEO: I am already reconciled.
FIRENZUOLA: We are successful when an accused admits his transgression and the justice of our judgment. Only then do we confirm the righteousness of our action, and strengthen the faith by abolishing doubts which a heresy has provoked.
GALILEO: So men must submit their minds as well as their bodies. Do you ask me now to renounce the work of my life?
FIRENZUOLA: Not so much. Only that you withheld knowledge of the injunction, and that your *Dialogue* is an argument for the Copernican system.
GALILEO: And if I do?
FIRENZUOLA: There would be no need to inflict harsh penalties or severe personal restraints.

ACT THREE

GALILEO: Tell me, Father, the decision, is it yours?
FIRENZUOLA: We recommend. Our recommendations are rarely ignored. In your case I have most weighty assurances they will be honored. Were it otherwise, I would not make this proposal.

(Galileo gets up, paces a moment, thinking, returns to the table.)

GALILEO: I will confess that I did not reveal the injunction, having carelessly forgotten it after so many years. Indeed, it still eludes me.
FIRENZUOLA: And the work?
GALILEO: On carefully rereading the *Dialogue*, I find, from excessive arrogance, intoxicated by my own cleverness, I wrote a book which contains persuasive arguments for the views of Copernicus.
FIRENZUOLA: How does your phrasing differ from mine?
GALILEO: It does not admit to deliberate perjury or calculated disobedience.
FIRENZUOLA: The distinction is subtle. Can it be so important?
GALILEO: I will confess to carelessness and neglect. I will confess to heresy out of vanity or ambition. I will, with my own hand, light the fire which consumes my books. But I will never make any admission that I deliberately, intentionally, defied the Church, that I have been other than an obedient Catholic. Not on the rack! Not on the stake!
FIRENZUOLA: It is enough. Let us prepare the confession for your signature. The Board of the Inquisition is assembling. Once we are done, I will take you there.
GALILEO: What will happen?
FIRENZUOLA: Nothing. Nothing at all. I will preside, and ask if you have prepared a statement. You will read it and submit the document. We will then prepare our judgment, and our recommendations for the Holy Father as to the appropriate penalty.

(*Firenzuola walks around the table, sits next to Galileo, who is writing, as the lights go down.*)

SCENE THIRTEEN

(*Galileo is seated alone at the table in his apartment. Through the window we see the dark of a moonless night. It is around 11 p.m. Galileo has just returned from a brief proceeding of the Inquisition, which received his confession without comment. He must now await final judgment, which, at the discretion of the Church, might come in hours or be postponed for months, even years. Although apprehensive, his fate totally committed to the obscure process of the Holy Office, he expects a judgment consistent with the pledges of Firenzuola, although he is pained by the high price of those assurances.*

(*Galileo has resumed work on the pages he was drafting when Firenzuola interrupted. He bends, wholly concentrated, over his writing, as—without knock or signal—the door to his apartment silently swings open. Pope Urban VIII enters, unattended. He wears the papal robes, but without the papal hat, exposing the thick, full hair which he, like Galileo, has retained despite his advancing age. He stands unnoticed, just inside the room, looking at the preoccupied Galileo, who, after a moment, senses a presence, and looks up to encounter the startling visitation.*)

GALILEO: Your Holiness! (*He immediately gets up and goes toward Urban, who deliberately, but not violently, flicks the door shut, turns toward him, and extends his hand. Galileo kneels to kiss the papal ring, then stands.*)
URBAN: You are comfortable here?
GALILEO: The apartment is spacious and wonderfully furnished.

URBAN: As befits a man of artistic bent. I supervised the decoration myself.
GALILEO: I am doubly honored.
URBAN: We have refashioned almost every chamber in the Vatican. Our sainted predecessor had many noble qualities, but delicacy of taste was not among them. (*He walks past Galileo to the other side of the table, briefly glancing toward Galileo's papers, and proceeds to a tapestry hung on the wall between the windows.*) Do you like this?
GALILEO: I have studied it carefully. Such fineness of execution. It is rarely found. The color, so varied, yet so subtly blended.
URBAN: Mercifully, a visitor with eyes. (*pausing*) Ah, Galileo, I am surrounded by such impoverished minds. See here, these threads, how precisely they define the border between the red and the gray, yet without interrupting the eye. A skill singular to the illustrious weavers of Gobelin. You recognize the scene?
GALILEO: Canossa.
URBAN: A favorite subject. The Emperor Henry IV—a startling likeness—prostrate in the snow at the foot of the mountain. Look carefully . . . the inclination of his body, his expression. One senses his trembling apprehension—wonderfully conveyed, perfect in its way—as he awaits the Holy Father's descent to receive his submission. That castle, where Pope Gregory waits, belonged to the Grand Duchess Matilda.
GALILEO: My ancestors served her in court.
URBAN (*turning suddenly back to Galileo, sternly, the warmth gone from his tone*): And what, do you suppose, has caused the pious zeal of Tuscany to decay?
GALILEO: No sovereign is more firm of faith.
URBAN: And his chief philosopher? Galileo?
GALILEO: Equally so.
URBAN: Why, then, does he wear a heretic mask?
GALILEO: I am he that you see.
URBAN: So much the worse. A heretic mask can be simply stripped.

But a heretic mind, a heretic hand, a heretic soul . . . these must be purged by the sulfurous wrath of God's own ministers.

GALILEO: If I have sinned, it has been through inadvertence.

URBAN (*interrupting*): Galileo Galilei, subject of Florence, vassal to the Holy Catholic Church, you have offended most mightily. Against Us! Against the Church you owe obedience! Against the faith you profess! Against Almighty God!

GALILEO: For writing a book. One doubtful volume, amid the works of half a century.

URBAN: Only a book! And the hemlock is only a plant. So Socrates was killed by a leaf. Your work is the greatest abomination in the history of Christendom.

GALILEO: I have submitted myself to the justice of the Holy Office.

URBAN (*in lowered tone, menacingly*): Were justice to be done— true justice—now, even now, your ancient joints would be parting on the distending rack, aswarm with such agony you would haste to the soothing embrace of the executioner's flame. (*He pauses.*) But you will escape justice. Justice is not in the interest of the Church. You are thought a philosopher. Men are not burned for philosophy. Your execution would alert men to your blasphemy, arouse curious minds, aid the progress of your heresy. You are safe from the stake. Unless, of course, you refuse to recant.

GALILEO: I will not refuse. Nor will I provide any future cause of offense.

URBAN: You will have no future. (*standing as if at his throne, in all the formality of his majesty*) Galileo Galilei, son of Vincenzio Galilei, Florentine, aged seventy years, I have determined that tomorrow morning, the twenty-second of June, in the sixteen hundred and thirty-third year of Our Lord, you will be conducted to the convent of Santa Maria sopra Minerva, and there, before the Sacred Congregation of the Holy Office, recite your confession—

GALILEO (*relieved*): Then you have already read the document I prepared with Firenzuola.

ACT THREE   191

URBAN (*slightly annoyed at the interruption*): And will renounce all false and heretical doctrines.
GALILEO: Yes. It has been agreed in every point.
URBAN: Furthermore. All works of your authorship are forever banned. Every volume of the *Dialogue* is to be destroyed. And any copies carried to the frontiers of Italy, confiscated and burned.
GALILEO: My works all banned! It was never discussed.
URBAN: Nor will you publish any further works. As to your person, tomorrow you will proceed directly from Santa Maria sopra Minerva, under guard, to your country home in Arcetri, where you will be confined until your death. To teach the gravity of your offense—and as a warning to others—scholars, professors, and churchmen shall assemble at the largest church in every Italian city to hear the text of recantation and the terms of penalty.
GALILEO (*stunned*): We agreed . . . the Commissary-General and I . . . we agreed . . . in return for my recantations . . . no further penalty . . . I was tricked.
URBAN: Discussed! Agreed! Is it a matter of commerce? Are we merchants? The Church of God circumscribed by contract? Defense of the faith, by a bargain? You were not deceived. Firenzuola spoke as he believed, moved—too much—by the honest compassion of his heart. It was not up to him. It was not for the Inquisition. The decision belonged to me. To me alone. He knew that. You knew. It is the law. The trick is yours, Galileo. It is *you* who have deceived *us*.
GALILEO (*resting his head on the table, then looking toward Urban, seemingly helpless to lift himself erect*): My name is erased from the book of the living! I detest remembrance of the time consumed in study! I despise every composition, and would obliterate the moment of their publication. (*He lifts the pen.*) I regret the very instruments of writing. (*He snaps it.*)
URBAN: Too late. It comes too late. Have you no remorse at the harm you have done the Church?

GALILEO (*a slight undertone of anger entering his voice, strengthened by the realization that there is nothing more to lose*): You have said it. (*pausing*) God knows that in this cause for which I suffer, though many men may have spoken more learnedly, none, not even the ancient fathers, have spoken with more piety, nor with greater zeal for the Holy Church.

URBAN: You dare! Before me! (*His voice then softens reflectively.*) I underestimated you. I have always underestimated you. A lapse of attention or imagination, perhaps. That first meeting at your house in Venice, an arrogant cardinal blindly in quest of destiny. It was your daughter . . . was it not? . . . so prematurely veiled . . . who bore it to the table, half enfolded in her holy robes. I witnessed an ingenious demonstration of philosophy. You, Galileo, saw God in a piece of ice.

GALILEO: I harmed no one. Perhaps I overstated the Copernican doctrine. An excess of pride.

URBAN: Do you truly believe it concerns the Church if the earth moves around the sun . . . if the sun circles the globe . . . or if every heavenly body—suns, planets, stars, comets, all—whirls about each other like some troupe of maddened dancers, all the while spinning and wobbling like children's tops?

GALILEO: Why else? (*He pauses.*) Is it the injunction?

URBAN: There was no injunction.

GALILEO: But the paper they showed me—

URBAN: Never issued! Commanded to destruction, preserved by a disobedient monk, whose willful insubordination came to serve a holy purpose. How infinite are the ways of the Lord.

GALILEO: Then it is the Holy Office which violates the law.

URBAN: The breach is yours. We observe the canon law lest our subjects, earthbound, untrained in mystery, mistake our obedience to God's commands for the willful verdict of vindictive men. Your penalty, excessive for disobedience, will not be equal to your sin.

GALILEO: The wrath of the ignorant . . . It was expected. But from

you, who could understand this new philosophy; the glory it could bring the Church?
URBAN: You believe that, Galileo? Of course you do. Honest self-deception, more dangerous to the walls of Empire than the artifice of Ulysses. You attend mass, tongue the communion wafer with untroubled mind, observe the prescribed devotions, and, I am sure, in your private chambers, kneel before the emancipating cross. You pray, Galileo, and murder while you pray. (*He pauses.*) To your penalty, I add a daily recital of the seven penitential psalms.
GALILEO: There is no heresy. I have not committed heresy. Here. (*He holds up the book containing the* Dialogue.) You will find no text of Scripture, no word from teachings of the Church. (*He holds out the book.*) No reference, not the slightest, not even an implication.
URBAN (*reaching forward, taking it with almost violent abruptness*): It *is* Scripture. It is, in every line, a work of faith, most terrible in menace to the order of Our Lord.
GALILEO: Your reading is the creature of your mind. All my labors, my life, solely purposed to understand His world, unfold the glory of His works, unveil the enormity of His wonders.
URBAN: Understand God! Glorify God! Demonstrate God! You? (*pointing toward him*) This ancient, enfeebled body. This age-bleached hair, squinting eyes fading toward extinction. A creaking man, helplessly confined by a small lock molded from the softest iron.
GALILEO: I have sought God's own truth.
URBAN: And found?
GALILEO: A little. Some small fragments, splintered from an immense construction . . . uncovered, not by revelation, but most strenuous application of His gifts.
URBAN: His gifts. Your senses? Your mind? Your reason? (*He walks toward the window.*) Come, Galileo. (*Galileo hesitates.*) Come. (*Galileo joins him at the window, a rectangular opening to the black-*

ness of the moonless night.) This window opens, does it not? (*Galileo nods; Urban throws the window open, Galileo starts back, as if in momentary fear, then resumes his dignified posture.*) Look down. What do you see?

GALILEO: Nothing. I know it to be a stone courtyard. The light is dim.

URBAN: Granite. Cut and quarried from Milan. At my command. Each stone required a dozen men. You might leap from this window.

GALILEO: A suggestion, Your Holiness? (*He smiles uneasily.*) I could.

URBAN: You have eyes to find the sill, limbs to bestride it, the will to jump. Eyes, legs, the faculty of will, all the gifts of God. Use them, Galileo. Leap and find the truth! (*He stares hard at Galileo, then turns back to the window.*) I advise against it. The fall might confirm your rules of motion. But at the end. Another kind of truth, mortality, which all the axioms of Euclid cannot explain. Man's faculties were given by God. It is undeniable. But the purpose, Galileo. You presume to know His purpose. It is not allowed to any man.

GALILEO: Except Your Holiness.

URBAN: Rarely. On most particular occasions. Never wholly without doubt.

GALILEO: Your Holiness has absolute command over the meaning of God's word, to consign the soul to damnation or absolve the sin and redeem the sinner. Power, even . . . perhaps . . . to make men believe. But you cannot change what is. The laws of nature. It is not in the power of any creature to make them true or false, other, than, in fact, they are.

URBAN: It is not our claim. It is not nature we deny, Galileo, but you. Your claim that man's mind, your mind, can enter the mind of the Divine; that man's truth, your laws, are also the truth and

the laws of God. If mortality can comprehend God, then Divinity is made a fable, and man is made a God.
GALILEO: Only the smallest fraction—
URBAN: None of it! Nothing! Nothing whatsoever. He scooped you from a handful of dirt, kneaded you into slimelike clay, formed you on His craftsman's wheel. And now, shall the pot understand the potter, the dust take wing against the winds? (*He pauses.*) You have a predecessor, the King of antique Sennar who thought to construct a tower to the Kingdom of Heaven. That telescope is your tower, the foundation of such a tower, aspiring to surmount this world. Should your philosophy survive—(*pausing, murmuring to himself*) Is there mercy enough in heaven for my sin? (*resuming*)—others will come, disciples, to heap new platforms upon the old, each stone disclosing new wonders, new laws, feeding man's agitated arrogance until it has swollen out the chambers of piety and doubt with certainty that they near the throne of God. Should they toil for centuries, for centuries of centuries, they will not reach His throne. The house of God is infinite, its chambers numberless, its knowledge longer than the duration of the world. Where, then, will you turn to know God? Will there be anywhere to turn?
GALILEO: Your Holiness, I hear, and I cannot believe what I hear. It is not you, but some fever of the imagination which speaks.
URBAN: Would you pray for my recovery? Should your philosophy infect mankind, the day may well come when your disciples, and, perhaps, even my successors, will pray for me. Their prayers will not parole my damnation. My Master has framed His judgment, and disclosed it.
GALILEO: To you, directly.
URBAN: To Sennar, the ancestor of your adopted ambition. In the very first chapter, near the beginning of the world, the tribes of the living all assembled for the mighty work. (*He picks up a Bible,*

opens it, turns the pages, thoughtful, unhurried, stops, points.) Here. (*He looks at Galileo and recites without once referring to the text, never taking his eyes from Galileo's face.*) "Behold the people is one, and they have all one language . . . and now nothing will be restrained from them which they have imagined to do." (*He closes the book, puts it down tenderly.*) Then, multiplying the tongues, He scattered them across the territories of the earth. Now, after so many years, you have finally come to undo God's wise confusion with a language—strangely compounded of numbers and lines and figures—which all can speak and read. Once understood, if understood, nothing will be restrained from them.

GALILEO: You read the ancient tale as prophecy? That God will again shatter our understanding and crumble the communities of men?

URBAN: He is no longer so intimate to our world. He will leave it to us.

GALILEO: I thought you understood. But you do not understand. This philosophy rests on faith. Our Catholic faith. The laws of motion, the language of nature, are all of His Creation. There is no other possibility. Condemn me and little is lost. Condemn the truth and you dim the glory of our Church, forbid it the knowledge which God has granted us to rebuild the ruins of our abolished world.

URBAN: *Would you have been a pagan!* Who imagined Satan so subtle, to come cloaked in the hueless robes of holy servitude? God's laws? Your laws, certainly. Nature's laws, perhaps. But God's! You do not deny God, Galileo. We are not threatened by denial. We are accustomed to denial. It is worse. You would make God unnecessary.

GALILEO: By revealing the abundance of His gifts? By demonstrating the laws He has granted us so we might understand nature and subdue it to our needs.

URBAN: You would subdue nature. Our duty is far more difficult:

to control man. You would understand nature. I must understand man, a creature of terrifying disproportions, a Divine spirit caged with a ravenous beast. In arrogance, comical. In submission, monstrous. Always at war with himself, and swift to war on others, pitiable and dangerous, hungry for belief, tempted to denial. A fragment of unintelligible tint, struggling to leap from the mosaic which alone defines him. A nature so misshapen is drawn toward salvation through most dread awareness of the hereness of God, shadowing each event and every experience of his mortal stay. Faith is the harness, and mystery the peasant fabric of our faith. You would offer a God of laws, a cause, not a presence, leaving the gift of reason our solitary guide to knowledge of His will. We are thankful for this faculty, but men are moved to worship not by gratitude but by necessity. And if reason alone is necessary, they will worship reason. (*Agitated, he paces the room, sees, on a small side table, the* occhialle—*microscope—which Galileo had presented many years before. He turns abruptly toward it, grasps it and carries it over to the large table, puts it down forcefully.*) Here. Your gift. To magnify objects. (*He goes into the adjoining chapel, reenters carrying a silver pyx, used to contain the host, and puts it on the table. Urban picks up a communion wafer and extends it toward Galileo.*) Here, the holy wafer of communion. Put it in your instrument. (*Galileo hesitates.*) I command you. We would have you observe it.

(*Galileo places the wafer under the* occhialle *and peers intently through the eyepiece.*)

URBAN (*impatiently*): Well, what do you see?
GALILEO: A pointed and uneven surface, most granular, like the face of rocks found on the side of Vesuvius.
URBAN: You do not see the body of Our Lord?
GALILEO: The instrument is not powerful enough to resolve the wafer into all its particles.

URBAN: Suppose a more powerful instrument?
GALILEO: There is none so powerful.
URBAN: Imagine it, then. Can we doubt that men like you will create it? Suppose, then, you looked and still did not see the body of Christ?
GALILEO: I believe in the sacraments. They are the heartbeat of our holy faith.
URBAN: You believe! When you were young you must also have believed in the Book of Joshua—that, to prolong the day, the sun stood still. Your belief will not bind your successors—raised on your philosophy, tutored by the God of reason. Unfortunately, they will explain, we are forced by the testimony of eyes whose light a benevolent God has mercifully united to our minds . . . to conclude that this wafer does not contain the body of Christ. (*He picks up the* occhialle, *withdraws the wafer, then dashes the instrument to the ground.*)
GALILEO: It would be an abuse of reason.
URBAN: It would not. It is a necessity of reason, consistent, logical, inevitable. There is only one flaw. It is not true. We cannot see the body of Christ because He is there. The absence. The absence itself is proof, a proof compelled by the sovereignty of faith over all the other gifts of God.
GALILEO: Is reason to be heresy?
URBAN: Of course not. It is a faculty to be treasured. Nor your laws. They are not heresy. Nor geometry. Nor the useful inventions spawned by your philosophy. It is your catechism that is your heresy. That man's truth is also God's, man's eyes gifted to pierce His mystery, man's hands strengthened to disperse the granite mist which enshrouds His impenetrable purpose.
GALILEO: So I am to be a heretic of logic. The first of his kind.
URBAN: You are not a heretic, Galileo, one who misreads the faith. You are the creator of a whole new faith, a heresiarch, whose trinity is the eyes (*touches his eyes*), the mouth (*touching*), and the

brain (*tapping his head*). A Galileo who encompasses the entire spangled world. (*He turns and starts to leave. Galileo is standing at the side of the table.*)
GALILEO: You are sovereign, the chosen vessel of Christ's earthly rule. Yet others are familiar to my work. More will come to learn. After I am condemned, Your Holiness, what will you do? Will you erase men's minds?
URBAN (*stops at the threshold*): If I can, Galileo . . . If I am in time.

(*Urban exits, closing the door behind him. Galileo sits, stares straight ahead, then picks up the page on which he had been writing, begins to study it.*)

SCENE FOURTEEN

(*It is the morning of June 22, 1633. We are in the large hall of the Dominican Convent of Santa Maria sopra Minerva, erected on the ruins of an ancient temple to the goddess of wisdom. The stone interior of the hall is white, built along lines and angles which have the austere purity of geometrical constructions. It contains no decoration, color, or images. The only color, other than white, is the red of the birettas worn by the white-robed cardinals of the Holy Office, who sit on a raised stone platform behind a long altar. They face the hall, where one can sense but not see the churchmen who have gathered. Suspended behind them is a large cross of white stone, clearly visible only because of the shadows it casts on the wall. No windows can be seen. The impression is not of a church or of the other rooms we have seen, but of a geometrical abstraction.*

There are nine cardinals [Francesco Barberini is absent]. Cardinal Bentivoglio, Chief Inquisitor, is in the center, with four colleagues to each side of him. In front of him, not yet visible, is a document.

(*There is absolute silence. After a moment, Galileo enters from the far side. He is clad only in the long white shirt of the penitent. He is holding a Bible. His body is bent, his steps halting, laborious, his appearance that of age itself.*

(He stops in front of Cardinal Bentivoglio, facing the raised platform and altar. With painful caution, as if trying not to fall, he goes to his knees, and lifts his head to the cardinals of the Sacred Congregation.

(Cardinal Bentivoglio picks up the document and begins to read. His tone is solemn, impersonal, official.)

BENTIVOGLIO: We, the Sacred Congregation of the Holy Office, by the grace of God cardinals of the Holy Roman Church, Inquisitors-General of the Holy Apostolic See, specially deputed against heretical depravity throughout the whole Christian Commonwealth, having cited you, Galileo, son of the late Vincenzio Galilei, Florentine, aged seventy years, to appear before this Holy Office, invoking the most holy name of Our Lord Jesus Christ and of His most glorious Mother, ever Virgin Mary,

We say, pronounce, sentence, and declare that you, the said Galileo, have rendered yourself, in the judgment of this Holy Office, vehemently suspected of heresy. (*Bentivoglio lifts his eyes from the paper and looks at Galileo.*) What say you, Galileo Galilei?

GALILEO (*shaky at first, but his voice becoming firm, yet still soft, as he continues*): I, Galileo, son of the late Vincenzio Galilei, Florentine, aged seventy years, arraigned before this tribunal and kneeling before you, swear I have always believed all that is held, preached, and taught by the Holy Catholic and Apostolic Church. But whereas, after I had been commanded that I must not hold, defend, or teach the false doctrine that the sun is the center of the world and immovable, and that the earth is not the center of the world and moves, I printed a book in which I discuss this condemned doctrine and adduce arguments of great cogency in its favor.

Therefore, desiring to remove this vehement suspicion of heresy justly conceived against me, I abjure, curse, and detest the aforesaid errors and heresies. Further, I swear to observe all penances that have been or that shall be imposed on me by this Holy Office. So help me God, and these His Holy Gospels, which I touch with my hand.

(Galileo is silent. All the cardinals have been gazing directly at him. After a moment, Cardinal Bentivoglio again picks up the document and continues to read.)

BENTIVOGLIO: In order that your grave and pernicious error not remain altogether unpunished, we ordain that the book *Dialogue of Galileo Galilei* be prohibited by public edict, as shall all other published works by the said Galileo Galilei.

We condemn you to confinement at a place selected by the Holy Office, and already known to you, where you shall remain for the duration of your mortality.

And by way of salutary penance, we enjoin that, for three years to come, you repeat, once a week, the seven penitential psalms.

And so we say, pronounce, sentence, declare, and ordain.

(Bentivoglio slowly rests the document on the table. He looks and nods to his left, and then to his right. The nine cardinals stand, file off the platform and out of the hall. One can sense, or hear, the sound of others exiting. Galileo remains, still kneeling, alone in the hall. Approaching from the side, walking slowly, comes Benedetto Castelli. He gently lays his hand on Galileo's shoulder.)

CASTELLI: Master.
GALILEO *(looks up at him)*: Good friend. *(Castelli starts to help Galileo to his feet. Galileo begins to rise, grimaces in obvious pain, sinks*

back on his knees.) A moment. (*Castelli stoops so Galileo will not have to look up to talk to him.*) Does Florence know?
CASTELLI: All Europe knows. Master, those who loved you before love you still.
GALILEO: It is beautiful in Arcetri now, at the end of spring. (*Castelli supports Galileo under the arms as he rises, very slowly, painfully. Galileo, upright, looks directly at him.*) Strange, how I misjudged. They did not want to change my mind. They wished to kill it.
CASTELLI: You will live forever.
GALILEO (*smiles for the first time*): Let us leave this place.

(*As they turn toward the door, they see Niccolini hurrying toward them.*)

NICCOLINI (*very agitated*): You are still here . . .
GALILEO: We were just about—
NICCOLINI: Have you any message from the Vatican?
GALILEO: Only that I am a heretic.
NICCOLINI: I could not bear to come. I had to. Better from me than from them.
GALILEO (*looking fearful again, still supported by Castelli's arm*): More?
NICCOLINI: During your absence, Maria's sickness was not abated. (*Galileo starts to say something, but Niccolini continues, hurriedly.*) Hearing of your trouble, she kept her own from you. This morning . . . late last night . . . the Congregation received a message from the abbess of her convent. In the last few days her illness deepened . . . she lost consciousness . . . they tried everything . . . but she died. Oh, Galileo, Maria is dead!

(*Galileo faces him, staring, his blank, uncomprehending look giving way to horror. He sinks again to his knees, conceals his head in his hands, sobs. Castelli and Niccolini rest consoling hands on his shoulders.*)

GALILEO: They have destroyed me! My poor darling girl. My only love. O God, Almighty God, why must she be taken from me? I am destroyed! It is finished! The story is finished!

THE CURTAIN DESCENDS.

EPILOGUE

(*In front of the closed curtain, to the left of the audience, on a plain wooden table is placed a device composed of interconnected glass tubes, partially filled with a pale pink liquid. Seated behind the table, working on the device, is Benedetto Castelli, grown old, but still recognizable as the man we last saw in Rome almost forty years before. The decades have brought him many honors: he has been engineering consultant to popes and to rulers of many lands, and recognized founder of a new branch of science [a newly fashionable label for natural philosophy]—from his day to our own, Castelli has been acknowledged as the father of hydrostatics.*

(A young monk, his manner serious, respectful, approaches.)

MONK (*pointing*): What is it, Master Castelli?
CASTELLI: Benedetto. Please. Benedetto. You are no longer my student. It measures the gravity of air. You did not know that air has pressure, as water does?
MONK: An invention?
CASTELLI: A suggestion from Galileo . . . many years ago.
MONK: You knew him.
CASTELLI: He was my master. He was the master of all philosophy.
MONK: Did you know his accusers?
CASTELLI: In those days I knew everyone. I lived in Rome. And Rome was the center of the world.
MONK: Did they ever regret?
CASTELLI: I was there, with the Holy Father himself, when the news of Galileo's death arrived. It was, I believe, in the year of Our Lord sixteen hundred and forty-two. Yes, that must be right. Isaac Newton was born the same year. You do not know his

works. They are not studied in Italy. But he is thought the greatest mathematician in Europe. (*proudly*) And a follower of Galileo.

Europe was in the twenty-fourth year of the great war.

(*The light on the table fades. The curtain rises on the throne room of the Pope. It is 1642. Graven by advancing age, Urban has become if anything more majestic—almost a monument of himself, his vital force apparently undiminished. Assembled before the papal throne are Magalotti; Firenzuola, now a cardinal; Caccini, become Bishop of Spoleto; Francesco Cardinal Barberini; Castelli; and François de Noailles, the young French Ambassador to the Papal States.*)

URBAN (*holding up some documents*): It must stop! The war must stop! There has never been such slaughter. Can you do nothing?
MAGALOTTI: All praise peace. None put down their swords.
URBAN: Europe is disemboweled. In the fields, desolation. In the streets, the living feed upon the dead. Our children cry out to us. (*He holds up a letter.*) From Germany, a simple peasant: "God send that there may be peace again. God in heaven, send us peace." (*He puts the letter down.*) Have we no answer? There is no cause to continue. No Catholic cause.
MAGALOTTI: The nations forget the habit of peace. Born in war, raised to the alarms of war, their only home the camp, their only work the battle, men fear the uncertainties of peace as men once feared the onset of hazardous war.
URBAN: Would Richelieu were still alive. He understood the uses of power.
MAGALOTTI: And helped return half the Empire to heretic rule.
URBAN (*angrily*): You forget yourself, Lorenzo. It was our policy too. Had we failed, our own states would now tremble before a Spanish Caesar. (*He points.*) Ambassador de Noailles. (*De Noailles steps forward.*) Instruct Chancellor Mazarin: the Church no longer

needs protection. Should he continue, it will only be to magnify the throne of France. We will renounce our support.

DE NOAILLES: It is not easy for one side to stop a war.

URBAN: Every month, every battle, multiplies the wounds which divide Christianity.

DE NOAILLES: Past all repair.

URBAN (*wearily*): That is for God to decide. (*raising voice*) Would France dare disobey! Before Us, there was no France, only usurping lords who chanced to quarrel in the same language.

DE NOAILLES: Now there is a France.

URBAN: And a Spain. And a Netherlands. And an England. And, soon, a Germany. God alone knows what disproportioned shape will be molded from that shattered soil. Shall each go its way, indifferent to the community of Christ? You invite chaos.

DE NOAILLES: I invite nothing, Your Holiness. I am only an observer.

URBAN: *We will have peace!* Remind Cardinal Mazarin: should this war continue past Our death, the Spanish will buy themselves a pope to replace this friend of France. (*De Noailles nods his acquiescence. Urban relaxes his posture, signals to a guard.*) The sketches for our new fortifications. (*pausing*) But first, Our nephew wishes to read a poem We composed last week.

(*At this moment the Swiss Guards open the door. Francesco conducts a brief, whispered conversation with an unseen messenger and reenters hurriedly, almost running.*)

FRANCESCO: Galileo is dead, Your Holiness.

URBAN: Another great man is gone. We shall follow him soon enough.

FRANCESCO: He will be buried in the church of Santa Croce.

URBAN: The remains of Machiavelli and Michelangelo . . . they also are in Santa Croce?

FRANCESCO: They are, Your Holiness.
URBAN: That would be a dialogue worth attendance. Galileo would soon be teaching perspective to Michelangelo and instructing Machiavelli in politics. (*The others laugh dutifully.*)
DE NOAILLES: His latest work on the science of motion is thought most important of all his discoveries.
URBAN: The manuscript escaped our guards. It was stolen . . . Nine years. Despite everything. He labored until the end. So remarkable a will in so dangerous a cause . . . Strange, the science of motion, is it? How things move? . . . We would have preferred to be less harsh. He was once our friend. We had no choice.
CACCINI: You struck a great blow for the faith, Your Holiness.
URBAN (*giving him a withering look*): It was as you wanted, was it not, *Bishop* Caccini?
CACCINI: Many shared my concern. Only you, Your Holiness, could have brought such a triumph to the Church.
URBAN (*rising, speaking with a strange, subdued firmness*): A triumph. (*his voice rising*) A triumph! A triumph, you say! I won no triumph!
FRANCESCO (*in a very calming tone*): I do not understand, Your Holiness.
URBAN: You never understood, Francesco. You will never understand. None of you will ever understand. (*There is a silence. Urban's wrath mounts.*) The man was nothing! The ideas were everything! A pestilence we hoped to quarantine.
FRANCESCO: And did, Your Holiness.
URBAN: And did not! The man's works can be found in all Europe. His ideas spread to every university, every court exposed to his infection.
FRANCESCO: They have no large following.
URBAN: Did not one bite from one apple corrupt all mankind? His ideas: almost irresistible. They instruct man that he contains, within himself, power over God's creation, power equal almost to

the Divine. Who can resist such deceitful flattery? (*His voice rises in anger.*) He fooled us all. We thought the matter finished. We should have known better. Even from his country prison, he never strayed from his ambition: through visitors, letters, the mysterious publication of old works, the clandestine publication of new works. He disobeyed us. He laughed at the decree of the Holy Office. His own solemn oath of recantation: nothing. A momentary concession to ignorance, easily given, easily discarded. He defied the Church! He defied the faith! *He* defied *Us!* (*Lifts his clenched fists and looks upward.*) *Bring him to us!*

FRANCESCO (*fearfully, but trying to calm his uncle*): He is dead, Your Holiness.

URBAN (*turning suddenly, his back to the assemblage, hands still upraised, loudly articulating each word*): **Would He Were Alive!** (*There is complete silence. Slowly he turns back, then raises his arm toward Francesco.*) Command the Grand Duke at the peril of his immortal soul, Galileo shall have no monument, his grave shall bear no inscription, from now until the end of time.